Integrated Marketing Communications:
A Primer

Integrated Marketing Communications (IMC) is here – apparently to stay! It is defined, managed, and practised in various ways. In this text, we are located in one stage or developmental phase of IMC. However, the text stretches well beyond this in terms of critical commentary and theoretical foundations.

The first introductory primer on integrated marketing communications available, this dynamic textbook combines the key foundations of theory with the best examples of contemporary practice, to illustrate how different aspects of integrated marketing communications (IMC) work together.

The book begins by setting the scene in which IMC has emerged as *the* major communications development at the end of the twentieth century and the start of the twenty-first. The authors explain each component of the promotional mix as well as the process of functional integration. Topics covered include:

- Advertising
- Sales promotion
- Direct marketing
- Marketing public relations
- Sponsorship
- e-communications
- Relationship marketing.

In addition to learning objectives, key terms, and discussion questions, the book includes a study guide and exam technique section. With key case studies on such international companies as Ford, NSPCC, Audi, and Pan-Pharmaceutical this book illuminates the practical side of IMC in addition to providing a clear and comprehensive introduction to the main theories of the subject. This textbook is a must-buy for anyone studying, teaching, or working in marketing.

Philip J. Kitchen holds the Chair in Strategic Marketing at Hull University Business School. **Patrick De Pelsmacker** is Professor of Marketing and Dean of the University of Antwerp Management School.

Integrated Marketing Communications: A Primer

Philip J. Kitchen
and
Patrick De Pelsmacker

Routledge
Taylor & Francis Group

LONDON AND NEW YORK

First published 2004
by Routledge
2 Park Square, Abingdon, Oxfordshire OX14 4RN

Simultaneously published in the USA and Canada
by Routledge
29 West 35th Street, New York, NY 10001

Routledge is an imprint of the Taylor & Francis Group

© 2004 Philip J. Kitchen and Patrick De Pelsmacker

Typeset in Perpetua and Bell Gothic
by Florence Production Ltd, Stoodleigh, Devon

Printed and bound in Great Britain by
The Cromwell Press, Trowbridge, Wiltshire

British Library Cataloguing in Publication Data
A catalogue record for this book is available from the
British Library

Library of Congress Cataloging in Publication Data
A catalog record for this book has been requested

ISBN 0–415–31420–8 (hbk)
ISBN 0–415–31421–6 (pbk)

To our wives Diane and Maggie
for their help, support, and
happy companionship

Contents

Figures

Tables

Case Studies

Biographical Notes

PHILIP J. KITCHEN holds the Chair in Strategic Marketing at Hull University Business School. Prior to this he held the Martin Naughton Chair in Business Strategy, specializing in Marketing at the Queen's University Management School, Belfast. At Hull, he teaches and carries out research in marketing management, marketing communications, corporate communications, promotion management, and international communications management. Prior to his academic career he worked as a manager for a national firm before entering higher education as a mature student. A graduate of the CNAA (BA[Hons]) initially, he received Masters degrees in Marketing from UMIST (MSc) and Manchester Business School (MBSc) respectively, and his PhD from Keele University. Since 1984 he has been active in teaching and research in the communications domain. He is Founding Editor and Editor-in-Chief of the *Journal of Marketing Communications* (Routledge Journals, 1995). He is Editor of *Public Relations: Principles and Practice* (International Thomson, 1997) and *Marketing Communications: Principles and Practice* (1999). He is co-author of *Communicating Globally: An Integrated Marketing Approach* (2000) with Don Schultz of Northwestern University (NTC Business Books, Chicago and Palgrave, UK); co-editor of *Marketing: The Informed Student Guide* (2000) with Tony Proctor (International Thomson); and co-author and co-editor of *Raising the Corporate Umbrella* with Don Schultz (Palgrave, London, 2001). His latest edited books include: *The Future of Marketing: Critical Twenty-First Century Perspectives*, *The Rhetoric and Reality of Marketing: An International Managerial Approach* (Palgrave-Macmillan, 2003), and *Marketing Mind Prints* (Palgrave-Macmillan, 2004).

Dr Kitchen has contributed to such journals as the *International Journal of Advertising*, *Journal of Advertising Research*, *Journal of Marketing Management*, *European Journal of Marketing*, *Marketing Intelligence and Planning*, *Journal of Marketing Communications*, *ADMAP*, *Journal of Nonprofit and Public Sector Marketing*, *International Journal of Bank Marketing*, *Journal of Corporate Communications*, *Small Business and Enterprise Development*, *Creativity and Innovation Management*, *Journal of Business Ethics*, and numerous practitioner journals. Dr Kitchen founded, organized, and chaired the First International Conference on Marketing and Corporate Communications in 1996 and was Editor of the Proceedings. This Conference is now an annual event. Dr Kitchen serves on the Editorial Review Board of the *Journal of Marketing Management*, *Corporate Reputation Review*, and *Corporate Communications: An International Journal*.

He has given papers on marketing management, corporate or marketing communications in England, Scotland, Czech Republic, Estonia, France, Germany, Belgium, Portugal, Australia, New Zealand, Spain, The Republic of Ireland, Northern Ireland, Israel, and the United States.

PATRICK DE PELSMACKER was appointed Dean of the Universiteit Antwerpen Management School (University of Antwerp) on 1 October 2000. He also teaches and carries out research on Marketing Research and Marketing Communications at the University of Antwerp and the University of Ghent. He is co-author of, amongst others, a textbook in Dutch on Marketing Research Techniques (1994, 1996, 1999, 2002) and a book on Marketing Communications (Financial Times/Prentice Hall, 2001, 2004), and has written chapters in various books on advertising, marketing, and management. He is Managing Editor of the *Journal of Marketing Communications*. He has published articles on marketing, marketing communications in general and advertising in particular, consumer behaviour and various other subjects in, among others, *Applied Economics*, *International Journal of Research in Marketing*, *Advances in Consumer Research*, *Journal of Advertising*, *International Journal of Advertising*, *Journal of Marketing Communications*, *International Marketing Review*, *Psychology and Marketing*, *Educational and Psychological Measurement*, *Psychological Reports*, *Operations Research Insights*, *Review of Econometrics*, *Journal of International Consumer Marketing*, *Journal of Business Ethics*, and *AMS Review*.

He has given papers, courses, and lectures on marketing, marketing research, and marketing communications in conferences and seminars in England, the Netherlands, France, Italy, Sweden, Poland, Czech Republic, Hungary, Roumania, Norway, Germany, USA, Thailand, Phillipines, Indonesia, and Vietnam. He is involved in executive training programmes for various companies and organizations on a regular basis.

Acknowledgements

The authors and publishers wish to acknowledge and thank the various individuals, companies, journals, and other authors and publishers that have assisted us in allowing materials to be cited and shared. Also, we thank the many practitioners and students who via their questions and comments have helped the authors sharpen and hone this work.

We express our acknowledgement and gratitude to Professor Lynne Eagle of Massey University, New Zealand who contributed chapters four and seven; and to Graham Spickett-Jones of Hull University who contributed the Appendix, 'Study Guide and Techniques'.

To all of you, thank you for your help, guidance, support, and encouragement as we offer this short work on the emergent subject known as 'integrated marketing communications'.

Philip J. Kitchen and Patrick De Pelsmacker

Chapter 1

Scene Setting:
Theory and Practice

LEARNING OBJECTIVES

After reading this chapter you will be able to:

- Interpret definitions of integrated marketing communications
- Appreciate the nature of integrated marketing communications and its multi-level layers of meaning
- Understand the approach we are adopting in this text in terms of its level of meaning and interpretation
- Determine how best IMC can be applied in practice
- Understand the shape, layout, and design of the text and how to make best use of it

KEY TERMS

- Integrated marketing communications (IMC) – definition(s)
- Integrated marketing communications – nature
- IMC layers of meaning

Case study:
FORD NO BOUNDARIES – MOUNT EVEREST EXPEDITION

The opportunity

Ford's 'No Boundaries' slogan celebrates those who overcome life's obstacles and turn 'no' into 'yes'. With its innovative media relations support of Team No Boundaries: Everest Expedition 2002, Hill & Knowlton showed that there are 'no boundaries' in terms of ability to generate brand-building media coverage.

To personify its No Boundaries spirit, Ford Motor Company brought together a team of five American women, all amateur mountain climbers prepared to stare death in the face and make a life-long dream a reality – scaling the world's tallest peak: Mt Everest. Ford provided the financial support and resources to make this expedition a reality, and Hill & Knowlton stepped forward to ensure that the eyes of the nation were following this incredible group of women, attempting to be the first-ever all-female climbing team to reach Everest's summit.

The strategic approach

Realizing the expedition provided a very compelling story and running drama, including team members who were mothers and grandmothers, ranging in age from thirty-five to fifty-eight who collectively had conquered physical challenges posed by cancer, heart disease, and diabetes among others, H & K cast a wide net for coverage including general interest, sports, lifestyle, and medical media outlets.

The objectives of H & K were to:

- Generate national and regional media coverage of the entire expedition from launch to summit.

- Overcome geographic challenges posed by Mt Everest to bring the Team No Boundaries story to homes across America.
- Create a strong association between Ford's No Boundaries philosophy, the Ford Expedition, and the incredible efforts of the team among the general public through in-depth national and regional media coverage.

The work

The programme was launched at the New York Auto Show, with all five members of the team free-falling from the rafters of the Javitz Convention Center around Ford's new Expedition to thunderous applause from everyone gathered.

Following a successful launch event, a *Today Show* appearance, and a national satellite media tour, the H & K team faced the greatest logistical challenge of their collective careers. With overwhelming media interest, how were they going to keep feeding the media monster and interested public with updates on the Team No Boundaries climb?

In its common applications, satellite technology provides public relations professionals a means of conveniently spoon-feeding news to the media and bridging geographic gaps from city to city. But when the hostile front lines of a Middle Eastern military conflict or the unforgiving terrain of Mt Everest are brought into living rooms across America, the value of satellite technology is awe-inspiring.

In order to accomplish such vast impact and reach, H & K's plan called for:

- Utilization of high-tech TH2 portable satellite equipment in order to provide live interviews from Mt Everest. TH2 portable satellite transmission units were secured in order to transmit live audio and visual signals from Everest for the purpose of live interviews with US broadcast outlets (these are the same units used by media in order to transmit live correspondence from remote and often hostile terrain such as the front lines of military zones in the Middle East).
- A streamlined process of capturing and transporting footage and sound bytes from the mountain to the USA.

3

- Use of satellite-fed VNRs as the primary means of generating consistent coverage of the expedition's various stages.

A system was developed and implemented by which weekly digital video footage was shot by team members and guides while climbing the mountain, transported down the mountain on yaks (that's correct . . . yaks) by Nepalese Sherpas (mountain men) to a DHL facility near base camp, and shipped to a satellite broadcast centre in New York City.

With equipment and personnel in place, H & K maintained aggressive media pitching throughout the expedition to national and regional media outlets, offering live interviews via satellite with team members from base camp. Most notably, NBC's *Today Show* and CNN were secured in advance of the expedition to provide exclusive weekly coverage throughout the duration of the climb.

H & K worked with broadcast centre staff editing weekly footage into four- to six-minute VNRs that were distributed to media around the country via satellite. Satellite media advisories were issued and aggressive follow-up efforts were made in advance of each satellite feed to encourage pick-up and coverage.

In addition to these efforts to generate coverage during the actual climb, H & K scheduled and managed Team No Boundaries media tours in New York City both prior to and immediately following the expedition.

The impact

- Weekly VNRs served as the leading vehicle for regular coverage, generating more than 400 media hits during the 6-week expedition. In addition, the VNRs were picked up on CNN's international feed each week, extending the story's impact to countries around the world. The VNRs averaged more than 80 broadcast hits from each satellite feed.
- Regular national coverage throughout the climb from *The Today Show* and CNN.

4

- National broadcast hits including NBC's *Today Show, CNN Live, CNN Headline News, CNN Sunday,* ABC's *World News Tonight, The Tonight Show, Inside Edition, National Geographic,* ABC's *World News Weekend* and *Good Morning America,* and on CNBC and Oxygen Network.
- Secured national magazine exclusive feature with *Oprah* Magazine. In a year that saw a record number of climbers (both individual and group) reach the summit of Mt Everest, only Team No Boundaries garnered consistent national coverage and recognition, despite coming up 300 feet short.
- Overall campaign generated more than 330 million media impressions equal to nearly $6 million in advertising value.
- Wire story from Associated Press resulted in print coverage across the nation regarding the expedition's launch.
- All resulting coverage included Ford's No Boundaries slogan, Ford's sponsorship, the Ford Expedition or testimonials from team members regarding the No Boundaries philosophy.

Source: Used with the kind permission of Ford, and Hill & Knowlton, USA.

OVERVIEW

Integrated marketing communications (or IMC for short) can be likened to the Ford No Boundaries case study. For example:

- IMC extends well beyond the promotional mix, though that is the major focus of this text.
- Media coverage can be, and is, generated and sustained by innovative and creative communication and media usage.
- Positive associations can be, and are, created by a relationship between – in this case – a sponsorship opportunity and the Ford philosophy.

The Ford/Everest case, and IMC present us with many interesting questions such as:

1 What is IMC?
2 Can IMC be interpreted (understood) differently – by academics and by practitioners?
3 What approach do we take to IMC – where does this text 'fit' in terms of meaning and interpretation?

This chapter will address these questions. Toward the end we indicate how the text will tackle them in terms of the rest of the book.

What is Integrated Marketing Communications or 'IMC'?

IMC is a product of the late twentieth century. Its birth can be traced to practitioner (advertising, direct marketing, and public relations) activities in the late 1980s – as witnessed by articles in the trade literature. Its growth can be traced directly to emergent academic interest, commencing in the early 1990s – spearheaded by the work at the Medill School of Journalism, Northwestern University, led by Professor Don Schultz. Since that time, its growth has been meteoric. But, like so many marketing developments, it has been driven by:

- Market dynamics (see Chapter 2).
- Continued academic inputs in the trade and academic literature (see for example the series of articles and papers in *Marketing News*, the main practitioner magazine for the AMA (American Marketing Association)).
- The fact that from its earliest beginnings, the development was embraced and supported by 'gurus' in the generic marketing discipline (for example, the top-selling textbook in marketing is by Professor Philip Kotler, also from Northwestern University).
- The widespread adoption of IMC by advertising agencies around the world, who were themselves driven by organizational exigency. Thus, ad-agencies are now integrated agencies.
- The apparent adoption of IMC by major companies around the world. Integrated approaches make sense to businesses, and to agencies who service their needs.
- The need to have 'promotion' appear to be consumer-orientated and consumer-driven, previously 'promotion' had been internally driven and by a philosophy of separatism where each promotion mix element had its own foci and dynamics.
- The need to overcome the 'silo mentality' associated with promotion mix singularity.

These dynamic forces are amply illustrated in the following chapters. But still we ask: just what is IMC? There are a multiplicity of definitions, and hence a multiplicity of understandings, and therefore potential and actual variability in terms of applications. Here we cite just a few.

Don Schultz (1993) stated:

IMC is the process of developing and implementing various forms of persuasive communication programs with customers and prospects over time. The goal of IMC is to influence or directly affect *the behaviour* of the selected audience. IMC considers all sources of brand or company contacts which a customer or prospect has with the product or service as potential delivery channels for future messages. Further, IMC makes use of all forms of communication which are relevant to the customer or prospect, and to which they might be receptive. In sum, *the IMC process starts with the customer or prospect and then works back to determine and define the forms and methods through which persuasive communications methods should be developed* (italics added).

The title of Don's paper included 'maybe the definition is in the point of view?'. He was right, the definition – and by implication – the application is in the point of view of the user or perceiver. The aims of IMC are:

- To persuade by means of communication (marketing and other forms, in fact all forms).
- To affect behaviour, not just attitudes.
- To start with customers or prospects and then to work backwards to develop effective communication.

Another prolific author Tom Duncan (2002) stated simply that IMC is:

a process for managing the customer relationships that drive brand value. More specifically, it is a cross-functional process for creating and nourishing profitable relationships with customers and other stakeholders by strategically controlling or influencing all messages sent to these groups and encouraging data-driven, purposeful *dialogue* with them.

Note that this definition is also focused on building dialogues and relationships between brands and customers, stakeholders, or prospects (see also Kitchen and Schultz, 2001). That dialogue or relationship is built, apparently, on some form of data-base – collected, collated, massaged, manipulated, and updated regularly. Messages depend for their validity and meaning on the extent to which the organization has correctly understood the buyer or prospects position, and created the forms of persuasive communication necessary to inculcate behaviour.

Schultz and Kitchen (2000) developed their own definition, repeated here for convenience. It resembles that of Duncan, and indicates the move toward integrated communication at the corporate level, as well as at the individual brand level:

IMC is a strategic business process used to plan, develop, execute, and evaluate coordinated, measurable, persuasive brand communication programs over time with consumers, customers, prospects, and other targeted individuals.

By this stage, IMC has become a strategic business process. It is not just about promotion itself, but about communication. Strategic refers to the overall driving force of the organization. IMC has become part of that driving force according to this definition, or — put another way — *it has the potential to become a driving force if a company takes the steps that lead to its implementation*. Yet, this book is not about strategy, it is not about a driving force, nor is it entirely focused on customers or prospects. Why is that?

- IMC is in the eyes of the beholder.
- IMC can be practised at various levels.
- IMC in terms of practice is still anchored to the dock of its very early stages of development. Staying with the analogy — some few vessels may have started out into the choppy waters of IMC, but many have not.
- New and multiple definitions of IMC may keep the theoretical waters hot, but only succeed in raising the temperature of a few marketing executives. Most prefer the less-involving, less-rigorously testing safety of the tried and tested.

IMC can be, in fact, what any organization determines it to be. It's most acceptable form is shown in stage 1 of Figure 1.1.

Can IMC be interpreted (understood) differently — by academics and by practitioners?

The answer to the above question is positive and in the affirmative. Different definitions mean different interpretations, hence different applications. Businesses are also diverse. They are each exposed to different market dynamics. If there is a new idea on the marketing street, an idea that promises integration, interaction, synergy, greater persuasion, at lower costs, with greater benefits — then that idea will be embraced rapidly, expeditiously, and its tenets supported and sustained within and without the business.

Figure 1.1 also crops up, and is discussed in greater detail, in Chapter 4 and typing in the names of either Kitchen, Philip J. or Schultz, Don into google.com will reveal a host of articles and commentaries on this topic. Note, however, that Figure 1.1 includes four stages, topped by the new and innovative 'integrated marketing'. Here, in this text, we argue that many companies, and the agencies who service their needs, are inexorably anchored in stage 1, some have moved to stage 2, fewer are in stage 3, and a handful are in stage 4. The reason for this apparent reluctance to move up a beneficial development path is simple — it costs money, time, and resources. It means relearning how to communicate. It means taking marketing itself seriously (see Kitchen, 2003). Most businesses do not. Instead, they adopt a simplistic half-hearted approach to marketing and communications which is characterized in two words: '*inside-out*'. That is, all it requires to implement IMC at stage 1 is a rather straightforward bundling together of promotional mix elements so that all messages speak, sound,

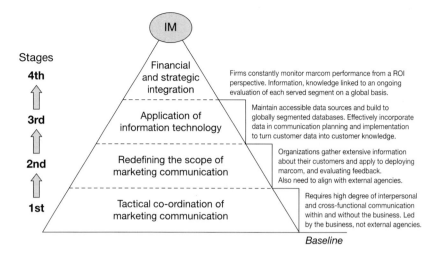

Figure 1.1 *Stages in IMC development*
Source: Schultz and Kitchen, 2000

or look alike, at least to receivers. Thus, to implement IMC at stage 1, means no real attempt has to take place to understand consumer, customer, and prospect dynamics (after all, that is an investment, a cost, and it means communication has to change from inside-out to outside-in). No investment has to be made to build and maintain databases or to apply information technology rigorously. No attempt is made to measure marketing communications return on investment, nor to ally marketing more closely with financial criteria. Let's take another look at Figure 1.1, this time with a slight amendment (see Figure 1.2).

What Figure 1.2 implies is that those firms who have opted for anchorage in the (for now) relatively safe dock of stage 1, may move directly to integrated marketing, without ever considering (perhaps that is harsh, maybe these have been considered but not applied in the realities of daily trade) outside-in, infor- mation technology or ROI. Put another way, for the majority of businesses IMC may never be anything more than ensuring that promotional mix elements – in essence – speak with one voice. Hence, most of the work in this book is associated with stage 1, or level 1, criteria.

The understanding and interpretation of IMC leads directly to application. Furthering that understanding requires study and learning. Applying increased knowledge requires financial and technological resources, and that precious resource of management or executive time.

For the sake of completeness, IMC – as a concept and as application – is now 'under fire'. Table 1.1 indicates positive and negative factors working in favour of and against IMC.

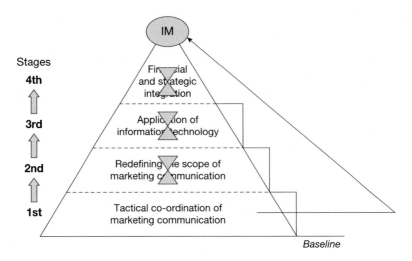

Figure 1.2 *The shortcut to integrated marketing*

Source: Adapted from Schultz and Kitchen, 2000

Table 1.1 *Factors accelerating and restraining IMC development*

Accelerants	Retardants
New integrated approaches coming to the fore	Questions as to meaning emerging
Offers key competitive advantages	Multiplicity/relevance of definitions
Underpinned by market forces – media fragmentation and multiplication – consumer/market demassification	Many discordant (dis-integrative) voices True progression with IMC is the exception
IMC now a 'watchword' or 'watchcry'	Many doubts and misgivings
Massive support from practitioners and academe	How to measure integrative campaigns – behavioural measurement only possible if business progress via four stages/levels
Still an emergent paradigm – great potential for growth and change	Many businesses anchored at stage 1
IMC theory and practice widely disseminated around the world	Possibility that majority of businesses at stage 1 may mean that IMC seen as simple to apply

Source: Adapted from Kitchen *et al.*, 2004

What approach do we take to IMC – where does this text 'fit' in terms of meaning and interpretation?

Our approach is fairly simple and straightforward. This text explores the concept of IMC. The text is located predominantly in stage 1 of Figure 1.1. It is deliberate. We do, however, provide a critical overview of IMC in this chapter and Chapter 3. We also discuss critical foundations of consumer behaviour in Chapter 2. Even the worst 'marketing' firm and/or its staff would benefit from information in this area, and they may move from stage 1 to stage 2 at some point. We also discuss – in detail – several elements of the promotional mix with a desire to inculcate thinking and practice. As this is a primer, we refer students desirous of further information on each topic to our major textbooks in marketing communications (see Kitchen, 1999; Schultz and Kitchen, 2000; De Pelsmacker *et al.*, 2004).

Let us see what happens, if businesses inadvertently practise unintegrated communications. In the November 2003 issue of *Director*, Carol Kennedy identifies three major communication flops:

1 The Union Jack on the tail-fins of BA aeroplanes were replaced by a series of outlandish garish designs in the 1990s. Notice, no consultation whatsoever with customer, consumers, or prospects. Expense and negative publicity – enormous. Result, project abandoned.
2 The new name 'Consignia' was dreamt up by the CEO of the then Post Office. Again, significant costs associated with name development, positioning, and communications were incurred. Employees disliked the new name. Consumers wondered what it meant. Consignia has been consigned to the dustbin of communication failure.
3 PricewaterhouseCoopers renamed its consultancy strategic business unit with the name 'Monday'. After just 7 weeks, and a £75 million cost, the new name, redolent with poor associations was abandoned.

SUMMARY AND CONCLUSION

IMC is here, apparently, to stay. It is defined and practised in various ways. Here, in this text, we are located in one stage of IMC though we stretch beyond this in terms of critical comments and theoretical foundations. It is, as we say, designed to 'prime' students to further studies in this emergent field of academic and practitioner endeavour. It may now be interesting to read the Ford/Everest case study. Where is this located in terms of Figure 1.1?

QUESTIONS

1 Access or download any recent paper on IMC from the Web. Using Figure 1.1, where is the author positioned? Can you identify a reason for that positioning?

2 Definitions are readily available. Compare an early definition (1993) with that from ten years later (2003). Develop a critique.

3 Is IMC likely to continue its forward momentum? Justify your response.

4 Identify two recent IMC case studies. How do these fit into the stages model?

Chapter 2

Integrated Marketing Communications

Chapter 2 provides an introductory overview to the topic of integrated marketing communications (IMC). For students and practitioners – the chapter will provide a range of tools, techniques and models that will inform, underpin, and help illuminate the individual disciplinary chapters that will follow.

LEARNING OBJECTIVES

After reading this chapter you will be able to:

- Appreciate the significance and importance of IMC as *the* major communications development at the end of the twentieth century, and start of the twenty-first.
- Understand the forces in the media and marketing environment that have moved businesses, and agencies that service their needs, to a greater use of integrated approaches.
- Recognize that IMC can be used at a variety of different levels or 'stages' by business of all types – for example, one level of IMC applicability is given in the introductory case study. It is up to you to identify the level.
- Note that the extent to which IMC can be applied is dependent on the business itself, not on the agencies that service their needs. Thus, integrated approaches are dependent upon where businesses and managers are. Many businesses are not just slow at implementing IMC, they are even slower when it comes to taking marketing itself seriously.

KEY TERMS

- Integrated marketing communications
- Causes of IMC emergence and growth
- Promotional mix elements and the link to integration
- Stages in the theory of IMC development
- Criticism of IMC

We commence with a case vignette. Though this case is focused on internal branding (in this case for an important subunit of the US army), it does illustrate where 'integrated approaches' may be now, in terms of application. Again, it is up to you to work out where this may be, using the 'stages theory' of IMC development.

Case study:
MAKING THE INVISIBLE, VISIBLE: INTERNAL BRANDING FOR ARMY MWR

Situational analysis/research

Keeping an Army ready to fight and win takes more than hard work and training – soldiers need a balance of work and leisure. US Army Morale Welfare and Recreation (MWR) provides hundreds of programmes and services that contribute to Army readiness by improving the quality of life for soldiers and their families. MWR represents $1.4 billion in total funding. MWR programmes and services are available at every Army installation around the world. They range from financial services, childcare, and preparing families for deployment, to recreational activities such as bowling, golf, yoga classes – and everything in between.

However, MWR can only contribute to Army readiness if soldiers know the programmes exist and participate. In an effort to drive participation and ensure continued congressional financial support, the US Army Community and Family Support Center (CFSC) approached Hill & Knowlton with a mammoth task:

To build and deploy a positive, unified brand image for MWR that would:

- Increase awareness and understanding of MWR programmes and services.
- Enhance the perceived value and appreciation of MWR, thereby driving participation among target audiences.

14

The target audiences included soldiers, their families, retirees, civilian employees, MWR directors, and staff – all Army employees in some capacity, but with starkly different job functions. H & K's mission was to communicate to these audiences the value of MWR so that all might take advantage of the services it offers, thus enhancing the Army's preparedness for war.

This case outlines the research and strategic planning phases of the programme, including a mini implementation on three bases, which led to the approval of a larger budget for final planning and implementation in 2003.

H & K began with an analysis of MWR media coverage and MWR websites operated by each Army installation to assess MWR's current communications style and messages. They also interviewed representatives from MWR headquarters in Washington, DC to gauge audience perceptions. Next, they conducted a brand opportunity assessment using secondary research materials (results from annual surveys, as well as focus groups from several Army installations worldwide). This assessment involved a thorough review of the MWR offering, audience characteristics, competitive framework, and challenges and opportunities related to both user demand and current communications channels.

H & K found that while MWR participants were happy with the services they use, non-users did not participate because they did not fully understand what MWR offers, where to go for MWR services, or who is responsible for delivering MWR. Many users and MWR service providers also did not fully understand the depth and breadth of the MWR offering.

The H & K team determined that these audiences' lack of awareness and mixed perceptions of the value of MWR resulted from communications inconsistency. MWR communications materials – from websites and brochures, to flyers and signage – differed widely in terms of messages, visuals, and overall quality. Each individual MWR programme or service communicated independently and competed for the participants' attention. Many MWR employees did not know about other available MWR services. And, because MWR programme availability, quality and service varied widely from post to post, perceptions were based on individual programme experiences versus participants' overall experience with MWR over time.

H & K also found that with hundreds of programmes at hundreds of installations all communicating *differently*, the messages were lost or diluted – failing to reach or to resonate. The net effect was that MWR was largely invisible to current and potential users.

Planning

To achieve MWR's objectives, H & K applied a strategically integrated approach to branding and communications to create an internal communications programme with the robustness and creativity of a *consumer marketing campaign*.

First, they built a language framework for establishing the Army MWR brand identity, which included a positioning statement, a brand promise, definition of the facets of the brand identity and message tracks by audience. Next, they built a phased communications plan including: perceptual benchmarks; rollout to Army and installation leaders; training for key spokespersons and designated brand ambassadors; and development of creative collateral materials and communications tools.

The strategy was to use creative communications to bring the brand to life on each Army installation — and 'make the invisible, visible'. The goal was to illustrate that MWR is an active, involved service provider — connected to audiences' lives — and make the MWR presence felt on the installation.

In light of the diversity and size of the Army community, the team proposed a pilot campaign to test the effectiveness of this approach before launching the new brand Army-wide. The initial $100,000 allocated to strategic positioning and planning did not include funds for executing the plan in the first year. MWR awarded an additional $200,000 to launch the pilot.

Execution

Three posts participated in the pilot: Fort Leonard Wood, MO; Fort Drum, NY; and Picatinny Arsenal, NJ. H & K designed a sequence of brand events to touch each key audience — a miniature enactment of the strategic communications plan.

Over a period of eight weeks, H & K introduced MWR's new brand identity to the environment and to audiences through a variety of tactics including:

- **Focus groups** to benchmark current perceptions, followed by more conducted in January 2003 to measure against the initial benchmark.
- **On-site briefings** with garrison commanders, installation MWR directors and marketing staff to build enthusiasm and support for the programme.
- **Programme manager rallies** as a forum to motivate and train the 20–30 individuals at each Army installation who oversee the delivery of MWR to be 'brand ambassadors', empowered to translate the brand message to their staff, so they in turn might better communicate the MWR brand to other audiences.
- **Voice/visual guidelines and brand kits** for installation Marketing Directors to ensure that MWR communications would 'speak with one voice' using a consistent tone, style and visual quality.
- **MWR mascot contest** — to engage MWR employees in a fun way, they were invited to submit ideas for an MWR brand mascot. One installation received over 400 entries.
- **Tri-fold brochure** for key audiences, which translated the MWR promise into layman's terms and embodied the new MWR brand identity both visually and verbally while showing the depth and breadth of its services.
- **Series of five posters** strategically released and placed in highly trafficked MWR facilities so that employees would make the connection between MWR

and their daily lives. Artistic imagery and poetic language ensured that they stood out as foreign objects against the backdrop of the typical Army installation.

■ **Advertising** in installation newspapers provided greater reach and reinforcement of the themes and images from the posters, combined with local information on where to find MWR services.

■ **Premiums** mugs, 'coozies', golf shirts, etc., all branded with the MWR logo and promise, reacquainted audiences with the MWR message at special events. Because MWR employees are rarely rewarded or recognized, a key chain/wallet with a special brand message was a meaningful way to show appreciation for their work.

Campaign outcomes

1 A positive unified brand image

The brand identity resonated strongly with key communicators at each site. They praised the overall campaign strategy, language framework, the quality, look and feel of the collateral materials, as well as the utility of the communications tools, such as the voice/visual guidelines. Each demonstrated their enthusiasm by making their own localized publicity efforts consistent with the H & K guidelines.

2 Awareness, understanding, value, and appreciation

Enthusiasm at each of the three sites surpassed the client's expectations. The pilot proved to be a valuable learning experience and a necessary step on the road to Army-wide brand launch. MWR leaders at each site agreed that reaching out to programme managers and staff was the most important part of the campaign. Many employees felt valued and appreciated for the first time. Program managers embraced the brand concept and verbalized their eagerness to improve the MWR 'image'. Their enthusiasm and buy-in set the stage for an emerging community of brand-aligned service providers, eager to share the value of the MWR offering with all audiences through consistent communication and service delivery.

MWR leaders also indicated that a continued branding effort would help them to:

■ Improve employee understanding of what MWR is and what it does.
■ Drive consistency in programming by clarifying who MWR participants are.
■ Enhance participant understanding of the link between MWR activities, and personal /professional well-being.
■ Increase participants' perception of value of the services and activities provided.

Because of the success of this pilot phase, Hill & Knowlton was awarded $450,000 for 2003 in order to complete the brand identity standards and implement campaigns to engage specific key audiences, including MWR leaders, communicators, and staff at each installation and MWR headquarters.

Note: Use of this material does not imply endorsement by the US Army Community and Family Support Center.

Acknowledgement: This case study is provided by the kind permission of Hill & Knowlton, Inc., New York and the US Army Community and Family Support Center.

OVERVIEW

This chapter explores the emergence of Integrated Marketing Communications (IMC). We consider the marketing communications elements with which this book is concerned including advertising, sales promotion, direct marketing, marketing public relations, sponsorship, the Internet, and World Wide Web. However, there are some omissions including point-of-purchase, exhibitions, and personal selling (see Kitchen, 1999; and De Pelsmacker and Geuens, 2001) for discussion of these). Based on this foundation, we then consider the development and diffusion of IMC in modern businesses.

Toward the end of the chapter, we offer a critical commentary on the current status of IMC (see Kitchen *et al.*, 2004). Undoubtedly, IMC or some variant with the idea of 'integration' at its core will be around for some time. But, if IMC is to make a real contribution, then it simply has to become strategic, not tactical. This means that business have to take a great leap forward in developmental terms, and turn from marketing rhetoric to marketing reality, i.e. – far more customer-oriented and customer-driven.

IMC – it's significance and importance

IMC is *the* major communications development of the last decade of the twentieth century Many organisations proclaim IMC to be a key competitive advantage of marketing. Integration of communications – as with anything else, attempts to combine, integrate, and synergize different elements of the promotional mix, so to consumers, messages through a variety of different mechanisms look, sound, and feel alike.

Growth factors

IMC emerged and grew as a result of the following factors:

1   Movement of marketing budget below-the-line – away from mass media advertising.

18

2   Media explosion and accompanying fragmentation.

3   Market demassification and splintering.

4   Greater segmentation and emergence of niche and unitary markets.

5   A revolution in information technology which is still sweeping the world.

6   More development of, easier access to, and usage of huge consumer databases that effectively underpin marketing communication of all types.

7   The importance of reinforcing consumer loyalty via relationship marketing.

8   The importance of building and increasing a brand's image based equity.

9   Generally, the brand was recognized as the primary driver of corporate success.

10 Development and diffusion of digital technology.

11 The spread of multinationalization and globalism, supported by economic and political means.

Driven by these propellants, IMC or integrated approaches to marcoms generally has grown, and will doubtless continue to grow, as we move further into the twenty-first century.

In the 1980s the concept of integrated marketing communications was unrecognized, embryonic, and emergent. Many practitioners and indeed academic commentators saw each promotional tool as separate and distinct, managed differently, budgeted differently, certainly not integrated in the sense that drove into the 1990s. Yet, IMC was *there*, underlying the surface, but few were trying to patch the disparate and early reports together.

Following the Caywood *et al.* (1991) report, and the significant work of Don Schultz, Tom Duncan, Sandra Moriarty, and many others, many academic commentators and practitioners started to jump on the IMC bandwagon. For ad agencies, it justified the move to becoming all singing, all dancing, integrated agencies. Moreover, clients seemed to want it. Clients themselves were driven by organizational exigency as previously discussed. IMC was here, but the emphasis was on making it work, not on what it was. A decade later, most firms are still there.

In the 1990s, a wave of studies – mainly with ad agencies – showed that IMC:

- Increased communications impact.
- Made creative ideas more effective.
- Provided greater communication consistency.
- Would improve client return on communication investment.

Yet, given the factors discussed before, ad agencies would say this wouldn't they?

There were some negative factors. By 2003, many commentators:

- Did not feel that IMC application could provide faster solutions.
- Spotted weaknesses in terms of effective measurement and evaluation.
- Indicated that IMC's time and cost efficiencies contribution were uncertain.
- Noted that much of IMC was concerned with the need to combine and synergise promotional mix elements (i.e. still at a very early stage of development).

Yet, as early as 1997, the flood tide of IMC development had turned most clients and agencies away from reliance on singular elements of the promotional mix. From then, in businesses of all types, agencies that serviced their communication needs, and from the pens of academic commentators everywhere, IMC was seen as the 'way forward'.

Marketing communications and IMC

Communication is the foundation of all human relationships (Duncan, 2002) and concerns exchange of information, ideas, or feelings. Thus, developing communications strategy requires extensive learning and coordination throughout a communications network (Gould *et al.*, 1999). Marketing communication is the collective term for all communication functions used in marketing a product. The purpose of marketing communications is to add persuasive value to a product for customers. Yeshin (1998: 3) defined marketing communications as 'the process by which the marketer develops and presents an appropriate set of communications stimuli to a defined target audience with the intention of eliciting a desired set of responses'.

Traditionally, the distinct tools of the marketing communications mix are advertising, public relations (PR), sales promotion, direct marketing, personal selling, and over recent years, cyber or internet marketing, and sponsorship. Each component has a specific task to achieve and the message is greatly enhanced if it is reinforced by other tools in the mix (Yeshin, 1998). These tools are adequately discussed in the following chapters. The elements of the promotional mix vary in their effectiveness as outlined by Fill (1995) who discussed the ability of each element to communicate, the likely overall costs, and the control maintained (see Table 2.1). Each element thus has a different capacity to communicate and to achieve different objectives.

Although marketing communications has been used for several years as an umbrella term, integration of these functional areas is what initially made IMC

Table 2.1 *Key characteristics of marketing communications tools*

	Advertising	Sales promotion	Public relations	Personal selling	Direct marketing
Communications					
Ability to deliver a personal message	Low	Low	Low	High	High
Ability to reach a large audience	High	Medium	Medium	Low	Medium
Level of interaction	Low	Low	Low	High	High
Credibility given by target audience	Low	Medium	High	Medium	Medium
Costs					
Absolute costs	High	Medium	Low	High	Medium
Cost per contact	Low	Medium	Low	High	High
Wastage	High	Medium	High	Low	Low
Size of investment	High	Medium	Low	High	Medium
Control					
Ability to target particular audiences	Medium	High	Low	Medium	High
Management's ability to adjust: the deployment of the tool as circumstances change	Medium	High	Low	Medium	High

Source: Fill, 1995: 12

a new approach to reaching consumers and other stakeholders (Duncan and Everett, 1993). According to Duncan and Everett (1993), a weak definition of IMC used by the American Association of Advertising Agencies was:

> a concept of marketing communications planning that recognizes the added value of a comprehensive plan that evaluates the strategic roles of a variety of communications disciplines (for example, general advertising, direct response, sales promotion, and public relations) and combines these disciplines to provide clarity, consistency, and maximum communications impact.
>
> (Schultz *et al.*, 1993)

The weakness is anchored in time. In 1993, IMC was still in its infancy, and tactical juxtaposition of promotional mix elements was all that could be entertained, *then*. Yet, IMC has since been defined in a variety of ways. Shimp (2000) indicated that all definitions include at least five elements:

21

1 The aim to affect behaviour through directed communication.
2 The IMC process should start with the customer or prospect and then work backwards to the brand communicator.
3 IMC should use all forms of communication and all sources of brand or company contacts as prospective message delivery channels.
4 The need for synergy, with coordination helping to achieve a strong brand image.
5 The need to build or strengthen brand relationships.

Indicative of so many other marketing activities, IMC appears to be defined by those who are implementing it. Kaye (1999) argued that the generally accepted definition of IMC is self-limiting because its focus is on external, non-personal communications: advertising, publicity, database and direct marketing, and interactive media. There are so many different definitions and ideas of what IMC is about and what it entails, right through to its implementation. Thus, the conceptualization of IMC is still vague and uncertain.

Yet, despite doubts and misgivings, IMC has become the dominant mode or paradigm for explaining how marketing communications works. Few writers, in either article or textbook form, could scarcely fail to mention integrated marketing communications.

The development of IMC

The idea of using various marketing communication tools in unison has now become the accepted norm. Its driving forces include:

- Information technology.
- The Internet and World Wide Web.
- The need for businesses everywhere to become customer-focused and customer-driven.
- Developments in database technology.
- Advertising and other agency practices.
- Globalization and the jockeying for global brands and global positioning.
- The need to improve organizational learning.
- More effective and efficient resource allocation.

Figure 2.1 shows that global and multinational companies can potentially use marketing communications in an integrated fashion to improve and coordinate their marketing communications strategies. The diagram presented is dependent for its validity on the extant national and global environments, life cycle stages on a country by country basis, the extent to which brands are managed internationally, and the corporate culture with regards to global or integrated communications approaches.

Figure 2.1 *The impact of global developments in marketing communications*
Source: Kitchen, 1999: 241

It was noted by Clow and Baack (2002) that to fully utilize the power of IMC globally, marketing messages need to be designed with a global theme in mind, so the same general message is communicated around the world. To develop a truly integrated global campaign, a great number of skills, talents, and capabilities are necessary (Schultz and Kitchen, 2000).

Schultz and Kitchen (2000) developed an eight-step integrated global marketing communication (IGMC) planning process. Through a stepwise methodology, each step is progressed consecutively in a circular process through a closed-loop planning system back to step one (Figure 2.2). The nature of this process allows for continuous learning and development of knowledge that can be constantly built upon as each phase is completed, and is an effective and market efficient communication approach.

Further detailed explanation of this model is provided in Schultz and Kitchen (2000).

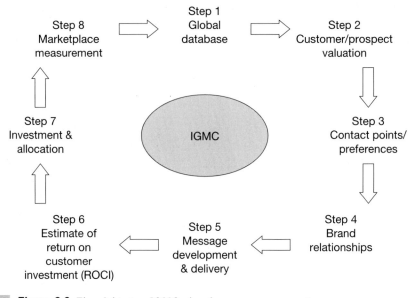

Figure 2.2 *The eight-step IGMC planning process as a system*
Source: Schultz and Kitchen, 2000

Critical excursus

The early literature indicates that IMC has stimulated significant interest in the marketing world, particularly when considering recent studies. The early work of Caywood *et al.* (1991) has shown that the majority of enquiries, philosophies, and arguments reviewed in this paper are around ten years old, making this a comparatively new, dynamic area of research that is still in an early growth phase (Kitchen and Schultz, 1999). Although there has been some scepticism in the past surrounding the value of an IMC campaign, 'there seems little doubt that IMC is an emergent concept whose time seems to have arrived' (Kitchen, 1999). On an ebullient note Kitchen (1999) proclaimed:

> IMC is a new approach to marketing communications planning being driven by technology, customers, consumers, and by organisational desire to properly allocate finite resources. IMC is still an emerging discipline and integration is a transition between the old historical product-driven outbound marketing systems versus the new information-driven interactive consumer focussed marketplace of the twenty-first century.

But, has IMC really conquered practitioners and the literature so easily? Has it been so readily absorbed by clients, advertising agencies, and public relations agencies? There are dissenting voices among the crescendo of chorused approvals. Even Schultz and Schultz (2003) identified some weaknesses in their latest milestone text.

Barriers to further developing IMC

Schultz and Kitchen (2000) identified four stages of IMC starting from tactical coordination of promotional elements, redefining the scope of marketing communications, application of information technology, to financial and strategic integration. They argued, based on the empirical findings from their research with advertising agencies which develop and implement marketing communication plans for their clients, that the majority of firms are anchored in either stage 1 or stage 2 scenarios. Some are moving into stage 3, but very few (a handful in today's world) have moved to stage 4 (see Figure 2.3).

Major questions here are: what are the primary barriers hindering the diffusion of the concept of IMC in companies? What are the major problems preventing further development of IMC in practice? And, what can be done to accelerate the implementation of IMC from lower to higher stages? Since IMC is to enable various messages from different communication channels coming together to create a coherent corporate and brand image, Moriarty (1994) considered the cross-disciplinary managerial skills the biggest barrier to IMC, while Duncan and Everett (1993) reported that egos and turf battles were primary obstacles to integration. Eagle and Kitchen (2000) identified four groups of potential barriers to IMC success in their study of New Zealand advertising agencies and the marketing industry: power, coordination and control issues; client skills,

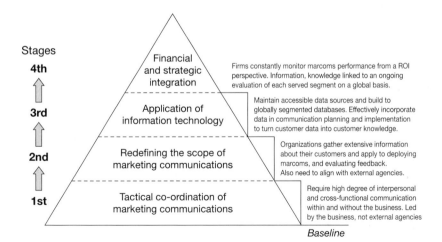

Figure 2.3 *Stages in IMC development*

Source: Schultz and Kitchen, 2000

centralization/organizational and cultural issues; agency skills/talents, overall time/resources issues; and flexibility/modification issues. Schultz (2000) saw structure – the way the firm is put together – as the most challenging problem of integration. He argued that the traditional command-and-control structures should be replaced by the quick-response model in new economy firms, and only when management starts to focus on outcomes rather than outputs do most of the integration problems go away. Schultz (2001) further noted that one of the problems with the current approach to marketing and marketing communications is the concept of a campaign, which is contrary to the customer-focused idea and the long-term relationship-building purpose of IMC, since campaigns generally are developed and executed for a limited time period – to achieve some type of advantage during a set timeframe. Although there are difficulties of ensuring the full integration of marketing communications and there are barriers of achieving final success of IMC, these difficulties and barriers will not be able to prevent people from trying, as the rewards of synergy and coherence are significant (Pickton and Broderick, 2001). Smith (2002) further illustrated the merits of implementing IMC: IMC can create competitive advantage, and boost sales and profits, while saving time, money and stress. A unified message has more impact than a disjointed myriad of messages.

Taking Figure 2.3 as an example of where IMC is, or could be located, *if* businesses have stopped their IMC development at stage 1, then this is stating no more than Cawyood *et al.* (1991) or Schultz *et al.* (1993) were saying at that point in time. Moreover, a stage 1 focus is what can be termed 'inside-out marketing'. It requires little or no focus on customers, consumers or their needs and is a relatively simple matter of bundling promotional mix elements together so 'they speak with one voice'. If is this indeed what companies *are doing*, it is a serious blow against the development of marketing in the twentieth century, for stage 1 implies product, production or sales orientation – orientations long thought to be receding into the sedimentary social and economic strata of the past.

Stage 2 of Figure 2.3 is at least an attempt by businesses to actively consider what customers and consumers want to hear or see, when, where, and through which media. It represents 'outside-in marketing'. It is a major step in the direction towards integrated marketing communications being driven by customers and their needs.

But, it is only in stages 3 and 4 that integration moves beyond juxtaposition of promotional mix elements, or use of market research, for in these latter stages businesses have to invest significant resources in building segmented databases. Only if communication resources are invested and measured against actual customer behaviour can financial returns be compiled. Thus stages 3 and 4 are a movement from attitudinal measurement to behavioural measurement. And only when we move to stage 4 do we arrive at a position which resembles integrated marketing.

Table 2.2 *IMC: different levels or stages*

Stages of integration	Critical
1 Need awareness for IMC	We assume this in our model
2 Image	Relates to message/media consistency
3 Functional	Relates communication to marketing goals
4 Coordinated	Consistency between sales and marcoms
5 Consumer-based	Relates to stage 2 of Figure 1.1
6 Stakeholder-based	Considers other stakeholders (corpcoms)
7 Relationship management	Coordinates marketing with other functional areas in relational terms

Source: Adapted from Sirgy, 1998

The real weakness of IMC is the weakness of firms to invest resources in the marketing and communication process. If that investment is not made, if businesses find themselves anchored at the dock of stage 1 or stage 2, then IMC will indeed have made a contribution, but it is not one of a strategic nature. It is instead tactical. And, yet, communication has to move from tactics to strategy. Only strategically oriented integrated brand communications can help businesses move forward in the highly competitive world of the twenty-first century.

Toward integration

Each and every element of the promotional mix can be focused on target markets, customers, consumers, and prospects, in order to bring about behavioural change. The theoretical constructs underpinning consumer behaviour (e.g. attitude, motivation, involvement, cognition, etc.) are explored in detail in Kitchen (1999). Sirgy (1998) suggested that IMC can take place at different levels as shown in Table 2.2.

We argue that need awareness for IMC is already well entrenched in today's global market. Our stage 1 (see Figure 2.3), automatically encompasses the attempt at message/media consistency and relates communication to marketing goals. Stage 1 also assumes coordination between all promotional mix elements and between clients and agencies. It is only when Sirgy mentions consumer-based that we start to move to stage 2 of Figure 2.3. In this text we discuss seven main elements of modern promotion:

- advertising
- sales promotion
- direct marketing

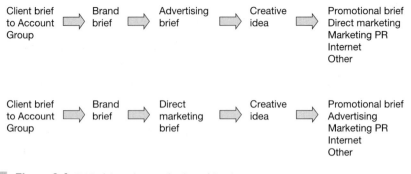

Figure 2.4 *IMC driven by marketing objectives*

- marketing public relations
- sponsorship
- internet or e-communications
- relationship marketing

and strive to relate these to the overarching IMC concept. Each element has to be consistently coordinated and juxtaposed via different medias so what is received (i.e. the message), irrespective of form or media is perceived by consumers as one message, i.e. a seamless web of communication. The medium, in our view, is neutral. The important element is communication via any or all of the promotional mix elements which then need to be integrated. Whether or not one promotional area takes the lead or not depends on the set marketing communication objectives. Figure 2.4 shows how this might work in practice between a client and an agency.

In all cases, agencies and clients are never presented with a communications problem, but with a marketing problem. That is what is discussed. To assume from the outset that the solution to all marketing problems is advertising is to make a well nigh fatal mistake. Instead a solution to a marketing problem may lead to a direct marketing solution, or marketing PR, or advertising. And, if the creative idea is good, then it will more than likely be applied in other promotional mix areas. For example, an ad campaign by Marks & Spencer, can easily be developed into related sales promotion, direct marketing, point of sale etc. That is what we are driving at in our argument in the next few chapters. We then revisit IMC in the final chapter.

SUMMARY AND CONCLUSION

This theoretical perspective has identified the various marketing communications functions, has located IMC conceptually, and has considered the value of IMC in the marketplace. A broader awareness of the IMC concept has been created and its reference worldwide has been explored. In addition, discussion has been provoked on the development and diffusion of an integrated approach to communication planning and implementation, which has considered the effect of technological advances, the value of databases, and the role of IMC on a global scale.

As we have seen, the concept of IMC has provoked diverse and extensive discussion. Although the subject is becoming far more widely accepted and recognized, there are still many ideas that are in need of further exploration and analysis, which can be done through extensive primary research. This detailed review of selected literature has provided an interesting consideration of how the IMC concept has evolved, where it came from, and how it is perceived in modern society. It will be interesting *to see what happens over the next decade.*

QUESTIONS

1 Why do the authors consider IMC to be 'the most important development in communications in the 20th century'?
2 Is the Army MWR case an example of integrated marketing communications? Justify your argument either way.
3 Consider any recent story from the trade press (e.g. *Campaign, Marketing Week, PR Week,* etc.). Can these be linked to IMC? If so, how?
4 Surely, IMC implementation can be done simply by orchestrating promotional mix elements harmoniously? Is this a weak argument? If so, why?
5 Why do the authors place so much emphasis on companies as primary developers of IMC? Should they be the primary focus? Explain.

ACKNOWLEDGEMENT

We acknowledge the kind permission of Hill & Knowlton, Inc, USA to incorporate the US Army case study in this chapter.

Some of the materials cited in this chapter are dependent on articles previously published in the following journals and appreciation is expressed to them to include these here: *Journal of Advertising Research; International Journal of Advertising; European Journal of Marketing.*

Chapter 3

Advertising

LEARNING OBJECTIVES

After reading this chapter you will be able to:

- Appreciate the scope of advertising and its role in the integrated marketing communications mix
- Understand how and why the role of advertising has changed, and will continue to change within the IMC mix
- Discuss the main criticisms of advertising and its impact on society
- Discuss the strengths and weaknesses of various advertising vehicles
- Understand the complexity of setting advertising objectives and appropriate evaluation techniques
- Debate how advertising works across a variety of markets and discuss the challenges in determining how its effectiveness can be assessed

KEY TERMS

- Advertising ethics
- Social responsibility
- Above-the-line; below-the-line
- Hierarchy of effects
- Standardization versus localization
- Accountability

Case study:
CONTROVERSIAL DTC ADVERTISING – XENI

New Zealand is one of only two countries that permit the advertising of prescription drugs direct to consumers (DTC). While it is an extremely controversial activity, DTC campaigns offer the opportunity to examine the role of advertising in fully integrated communications campaigns. Xenical, a prescription-only weight reduction product used only for severe obesity, is marketed by Hoffman La Roche Ltd internationally. In New Zealand, the company is represented by Roche Products (NZ) Ltd. Xenical has a high level of product differentiation from competitive weight reduction products. The challenge for Roche Products in New Zealand was to develop a DTC promotional campaign for Xenical within the complex and restrictive provisions of the New Zealand legal and regulatory system. Several possible themes were pre-tested and the theme that scored highest in terms of likeability and matching consumer needs was developed into an integrated campaign with the following central theme:

Lose weight. Gain life.

Health professionals were provided with a preview of the consumer advertising campaign immediately prior to the consumer launch. Thereafter, consumer advertising ran in tandem with activity targeted at doctors and pharmacists. A combination of PR, direct mail, workshops/seminars, and professional press was used to communicate with health professionals. The consumer campaign launched with a television teaser campaign in May 1998.

On 2 June, countless New Zealanders will finally get the help they have been waiting for.

This was followed by the main consumer campaign in June 1998, using a combination of television, print, radio, and PR. Extensive editorial coverage was gained. The focus of the campaign communication then moved to costs, programme details, and the efficacy of the Xenical programme. A key element of the Xenical promotional programme is the *Xenical Weight Management Programme* that includes a weight-control diary and healthy eating and nutritional advice. An additional element is a free (0800) support line, the number for which is provided only by doctors or pharmacists when Xenical is prescribed by a doctor/prescription filled at a pharmacy.

An extension of this support line is the facility for health professionals to maintain contact, subject to agreement, with those on the programme to identify potential problems, and to provide advice, motivation, and monitoring support. Additional elements for the Weight Management Programme included magazines and mentor groups in the form of community meetings and workshops. Sales targets were exceeded

31

by over 200 per cent in 1999, and a 20 per cent share of the estimated NZ $100 million weight control market was gained. Brand awareness reached 81 per cent by the end of August 1999 and research showed 89 per cent of doctors had prescribed Xenical since its launch, with the main reason for prescribing (48 per cent) being patient requests.

Source: Case study data sourced from Meares Taine Limited, and reproduced with permission.

While DTC itself is an extremely controversial activity, primarily for its impact on doctor–patient relationships, the Xenical case illustrates how advertising can play a significant role in an integrated marketing communication campaign, not just in creating awareness, but also motivating actual behavioural change.

OVERVIEW

This chapter begins by reviewing the scope of advertising and the way in which its role has changed in the last twenty years. The main criticisms of advertising and its assumed impact on society are then discussed. This is followed by a discussion of the complexities of determining how advertising actually works, what it can be expected to achieve and how its effectiveness can, or should, be measured.

Advertising's changing face: its scope and changing role in the integrated marketing communications mix

Many texts give a long-held standard definition of advertising as 'any paid form of non-personal presentation of ideas, goods or services by an identified sponsor' (Berkman and Gilson, 1987: 9). It is seen as fulfilling one or more of the following communications functions: informing, persuading, reminding, adding value, and assisting other company efforts (Shimp, 2003: 231), the relative importance of each function being dependent on the communication objectives of the specific situation.

Advertising is perceived as a modern activity, but has its first recorded origins in simple signage and verbal (shouted) messages some 3,000 years BC (Berkman and Gilson, 1987). In terms of 'modern' (the last century), most advertising was print based prior to the 1920s; radio then became the 'new' technology, bringing with it concerns regarding its power and influence:

The popularity of this new pastime among children has increased rapidly . . . This new invader of the privacy of the home has brought many a disturbing influence in its wake. Parents have become aware of a puzzling change in the behaviour pattern of their children. They are bewildered by a host of new problems, and find themselves unprepared, frightened, resentful, helpless. They cannot lock out this intruder because it has gained an invincible hold of their children.

(Eisenberg, 1936 – discussing the impact of radio)

Television began in the 1930s, but did not become a mass commercial medium until 1950. It remained the dominant commercial medium until the 1990s, when a combination of media fragmentation, new electronic technology, and sophisticated database management tools allowed more precise targeting and greater cost efficiency, causing budgets to move away from mass media into more tightly segmented and targeted options such as direct mail. These developments, in fact, saw the share of marketing communication budget allocated to all forms of mass media ('above-the-line') decline substantially with increasing amounts of expenditure being moved to 'below-the-line' activities such as sales promotions. Note: the distinction between above- and below-the-line is an historical one. Advertisers used to pay their advertising agencies commission on mass media placement, not

Table 3.1 *Traditional above-the-line versus below-the-line advertising*

Traditional media

Television	
Radio	
Newspaper	
Magazine	
Cinema	Commission bearing
Directory advertising (e.g. 'Yellow Pages')	
Some forms of outdoor signage (e.g. static hoardings)	
Direct mail	
Sales promotions (although this may involve using other media forms)	Non-commission bearing – now usually negotiated on a fee for service basis
Brochures, flyers etc.	

New media forms

Internet	
Product placement in movies and in television programmes	Usually negotiated on a fee for service basis
Videotapes/CD-Roms	
Event signage (including computer-generated 'virtual' signage and holograms)	
Flexible forms of outdoor signage such as advertising on cars, taxis, yacht sails, balloons	

on other communications activity. A line was drawn on schedules and invoices to denote the cut-off point. Table 3.1 illustrates the distinction between the two.

Advertising accountability

The move away from mass media occurred at a time when increased competitiveness between advertising agencies was coupled with calls from clients to justify advertising expenditure and to demonstrate the effects and effectiveness of advertising campaigns (Flandin *et al.*, 1992). The difficulty of measuring the real impact of advertising and thus justifying expenditure led to budgets being cut when markets were tight in order to maintain bottom line returns. The advertising sector has become painfully aware that:

> there are no willing advertisers. Each time the decision is made to spend more money on advertising, it is only because the manufacturer or retailer does not know of a more efficient, more economical way of generating sales of his product.
>
> (Flandin *et al.*, 1992: 204)

The question of accountability and remuneration for advertising agencies has been a hotly debated area. For many years, the commission gained by advertising agencies working on behalf of their clients was made up of 15 per cent true commission and a further 5 per cent for prompt payment of their accounts with the various media. In addition, invoices from suppliers were 'grossed up' by the same amount, i.e. commission was placed on the incoming amount and the higher fee charged to the client. This system began to break down in the mid-1980s and a number of systems now operate, ranging from various commission levels – now closer to 10 per cent on average than the old 20 per cent – to fees for services or a negotiated flat fee. An interesting variation on this is from Procter & Gamble. The material shown opposite is taken from a press release issued by the organization in late 1999 (reproduced with permission of Procter & Gamble).

A more moderate variation on the Procter & Gamble system is the provision of a performance bonus for advertising agencies, in addition to whatever compensation structure is in place. The bonus is linked to client sales performance – or other negotiated criteria set as objectives at the start of a financial year or campaign period.

The pressures on traditional advertising agencies in terms of declining shares of marketing communications budgets and declining revenues from their activity means that they have been forced to re-evaluate their role within the wider marketing communication mix. Strategies such as expanding services offered to incorporate other marketing communications functions and/or strategic alliances

PROCTER & GAMBLE MOVES TO A SALES-BASED COMPENSATION SYSTEM

Effective 1 July, 2000, P&G will pay its advertising agencies a percentage of global brand sales, versus today's commission based on media spending. The new sales-based compensation model aligns agency growth with P&G growth, encourages holistic, media-neutral marketing, and compensates based on global results. 'Our overarching objective is to increase top line sales growth', says Bob Wehling, P&G's global marketing officer. 'We and our agencies are convinced that this new compensation system will keep us focused on achieving that goal'.

'This change in the way we are compensated reinforces our shared commitment to increase P&G's sales growth and helps stimulate the continued growth of their advertising agency partners', comments Kevin Roberts, chief executive officer, Saatchi & Saatchi.

Growth based compensation

The new system closely aligns agency compensation to P&G sales by tying its compensation structure to each brand's total annual sales. It is intended to reward agencies for driving global top-line growth. 'By increasing our focus to building large brands, we will apply our resources towards those projects having the greatest potential for strengthening the business to the benefit of P&G and its agencies', said Roger Haupt, incoming president, and chief executive officer, Leo Burnett.

'It's really simple: As we grow, our agencies grow', added Wehling. 'I can't think of a better way to align around common objectives. It will simplify our efforts and keep us all focussed on the end goal – increased brand sales'.

Holistic, media neutral marketing

P&G's current compensation system rewards its agencies based on a straight percentage of total media spending. This leads to marketing plans that are heavily skewed towards traditional media. 'The old system has its inherent flaws – plans tend to favour television and print to the exclusion of the Internet, direct mail and other options,' says Ed Meyer, chairman and chief executive officer, Grey Advertising, Inc. 'With this new system, we will be encouraged to create holistic marketing plans that drive the growth of our brands. Our rewards will be based not on which media we used, but on successful business-building ideas and programs'.

Global planning

Consistent with P&G's Organization 2005 restructuring, this system will compensate agencies globally. 'This new structure empowers us to better align our talent and resources, break down geographic barriers and focus on global growth of P&G's brands', explains Arthur Selkowitz, chairman and chief executive officer of D'Arcy Masius, Benton & Bowles.

Collective effort

The new system results from a collaborative effort between P&G and its agencies, aimed at ensuring both are positioned for success in the changing media and marketing environment.

The change to the compensation system follows a significant adjustment to P&G's agency conflict policy, which was effective 1 January, 1999. The new policy is less restrictive and gives P&G agencies more opportunity to grow their business with all clients. 'We want our agencies to be as strong as possible so that the best talent in the world can be hired to work on our business', says Wehling.

'We love this change', comments Pat McGrath, chairman and chief executive officer, Jordan McGrath Case & Partners/EURO RSCG. 'It's all about increasing agency revenues as a result of bigger, better business building ideas and not just bigger media budgets. Hallelujah!'

with other communications sectors have created tensions, particularly within the public relations sector that see their specialist functions being usurped (Ewing *et al.*, 2000).

Advertising media

Kotler (1980) illustrates the extent of media options twenty years ago by listing main media choices as newspapers, television, magazines, direct marketing, radio, magazines and outdoors. He restricted their evaluation to issues of reach, frequency and impact. His list of media options in 2000 had almost doubled, to include consideration of packaging along with new electronic media, together with combinations of advertising and editorial ('advertorials'/'infomercials') as well as product placements within movies. Somewhat surprisingly, his discussion of evaluation and effectiveness remained largely as outlined twenty years prior (Kotler, 2000).

Each medium has its own set of unique strengths and weaknesses, both as stand-alone options and in tandem with other media. Consider the ability of

Table 3.2 Example of media strengths and weaknesses: television

Strengths	Weaknesses
High reach	Expensive
Ability to combine sight and sound/ demonstrate	Short duration (30 seconds is usually time for only 75 words) – no opportunity to refer back to the message
Ability to portray emotion and excitement	Clutter and high levels of competitive activity
Credibility	Difficult to regionalize
Able to provide reminders close to likely purchase period	

television to communicate sight, sound, movement and emotion against the limitations of a short time period (see Table 3.2). Then contrast it to radio, newspapers, magazines, or any of the newer media vehicles. Also consider the environment in which the advertising may be seen and whether the intended receiver is receptive or likely to pay only partial attention to the advertising (see Figure 3.1). Also consider how easily people can avoid advertising (turning the page of print media, changing channels, or muting television). Breaking through the increasing clutter of competing advertising is a major challenge for advertisers. The advent of new media forms such as digital television will bring new challenges for advertisers who will need to adapt and to devise means of communicating to consumers via media options that are, as yet, only poorly understood.

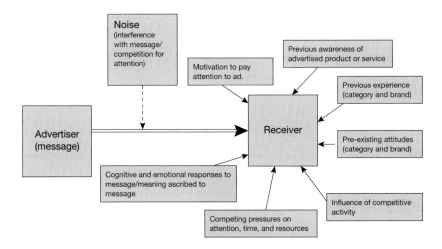

Figure 3.1 Advertising does not appear in isolation

Message and meaning, global and cultural challenges

Further challenges to advertising effectiveness have emerged in the last decade, particularly in relation to growing globalization of markets and the need to consider cross-cultural communication and to understand the extent to which advertising can be standardized across national borders versus being localized to meet the requirements and preferences of specific markets. Standardization of advertising can also assist in brand image consistency across markets (see Kotabe and Helsen, 1998). It also offers considerable economies of scale. However, even when similar campaigns are used across multiple countries, international differences in culture, legal and/or regulatory requirements may mean that one or more element of the advertisement may be required to be tailored to local conditions to be effective, or legal (see Boyd et al., 1998).

In addition, cultural differences lead to different expectations of, and attitudes towards, advertising. For example, Japanese prefer emotion-based soft sell whereas Europeans and Americans prefer logic and more direct selling approaches (Hennessey, 1998). Further, signs, symbols, colours, and numbers often have very different meanings across cultures. In fact, in any individual culture, multiple meanings may be taken from advertising – or any other form of communication. Although an advertiser may intend a central meaning, individuals may draw on different resources and generate new meanings. Increasingly, the persuasive appeal of a commercial hinges on effectively integrating relevant imagery from popular culture and whether the interpreted message has resonance with consumers' lifestyles and dreams, rather than on the literal and factual content of the message. (Bulmer and Buchanan-Oliver, 2004). The challenge for advertisers working across national boundaries and across cultures, centres on understanding the consumer target and tailoring appropriate advertising messages that will reward the attention being sought for them. This includes considering the degree of localization that should be, or is required to be, undertaken in order for the advertising to not only meet regulatory requirements but also to ensure that the message consumers take from the advertisements is compatible with what was intended by the advertiser.

Advertising ethics and social responsibility

Mass media communication, especially advertising, has been criticized internationally over a long period of time for being deceptive, manipulative, offensive, and for influencing people to buy products or services they do not need (Shimp, 2003). However, advertising's supporters counter many of these criticisms, suggesting that consumers believe it provides valuable information and that its benefits outweigh the shortcomings that consumers understand and take into account (Calfee and Ringold, 1994). Economic arguments regarding the positive social value of advertising have been made for many years (Telser, 1964; Benham, 1972) and centre on: reduced search and information costs to consumers arising from advertising; higher sales of advertised products leading to economies of scale and lower prices (if the advertiser's monopoly power does not operate to the contrary); advertising resulting in an increased price elasticity of demand for the advertised products in contrast to the price inelasticity of demand exhibited by lesser advertised products; and the level of advertising acting as a signal for quality.

Despite this, advertising currently faces major threats that could potentially lead to wide-ranging restrictions, if not outright bans. The rationale for proposed advertising restrictions is underpinned by claimed social ill-effects of advertising. It is claimed that – in some cases – advertising creates harmful health effects. This argument has centred principally on controversy surrounding tobacco advertising, especially campaigns that target young (potential) smokers. Bans on advertising tobacco products are now in place in many countries. The focus has now moved to the advertising of food products, with claims of direct links between advertising, unhealthy dietary habits, and obesity (French et al., 2001; McLellan, 2002) which culminated in an unsuccessful attempt to sue McDonald's Restaurants for failing to warn consumers of health dangers claimed to be associated with consuming their food (Buchholz, 2003). More broadly, advertising is also criticized for contributing to the broader issue of consumerism, creating a materialistic, consumerist mentality, which has environmentally damaging implications (Kirkpatrick, 1986; Denny, 1999; Higham, 1999).

There is an implied, simplistic, direct cause and effect relationship in these criticisms – that advertising is the direct cause of a range of complex societal problems. The assumption appears to be that these problems will be removed through the imposition of bans on advertising – the most visible and accessible form of external influence (Higham, 1999). Governments are under pressure to be seen to act on constituents' concerns – restricting advertising to a group seen as particularly vulnerable to marketing manipulation may seem an easy way to show that the government takes such issues seriously. The efficacy of such actions is dubious. A major 1996 British study undertaken for the Ministry of Agriculture, Fisheries and Food (Young and Webley, 1996) suggests that there is no evidence that advertising is the (or even 'a') principal influence on children's eating behaviours. In addition, the study stressed that there is no serious and methodologically sound evidence that shows that food advertising leads to an increase in the consumption by children of whole categories of food. However, advertisers must assume high standards of social responsibility, particularly in directing messages at children, a group seen as particularly vulnerable to persuasion due to their limited cognitive development (McCall, 1999; Preston, 2000).

It's not what advertising does to people – it's what people do with advertising

Much of the assumptions regarding advertising's effects are based on the assumption that advertising is a strongly persuasive force. Consumers are not, however, passive recipients of advertising messages. Lannon (1996: 24) suggests that the question is no longer 'what does advertising do?' a question she and others raised over a decade ago, but rather 'what do people do with advertising?'.

The perception of advertising as a strong force originates from a long-held view (Barry, 1987) that advertising works via a 'hierarchy of effects'. This concept originated a century ago and envisages consumers moving through a series of stages from initial awareness of a product (A), through exposure to its advertising, to interest in the product (I), desire for the product (D), and finally action (A) in terms of purchase behaviour (the AIDA model). For an in-depth review of the strengths and weaknesses of such models, see Barry and Howard, 1990.

AIDA is criticized as unproven and too simplistic (Shankar, 1999), yet it remains a central tenet of many marketing texts. Indeed, the view of advertising as a strongly persuasive force in all market sectors remains a major theme in both academic and practitioner literature, particularly that originating from the USA (Churchill and Peter, 1998; Perrault and McCarthy, 1999; Kotler, 2000). It has maintained its dominance in spite of challenges launched over almost thirty years (Ehrenberg *et al.*, 1997). The lengthy battle for recognition that the 'strong force' does not apply to all market sectors is well documented by Jones (1990) and supported by Ambler (2000: 299) who observes:

> The assumption that advertising equals persuasion is so ingrained in the USA that to challenge it elicits much the same reaction as questioning your partner's parentage.

Helgesen (1996) claims that a great deal of advertising has a weak impact on consumers. Heath (2001) endorses this, suggesting that, for low involvement products, there is an expectation that familiar brands in a product category will be similar in performance to each other and that there is therefore minimal incentive for consumers to pay attention to advertising for these brands. Ambler (2000) also criticizes both the traditional hierarchy of effects models such as AIDA and more recent variations such as that proposed by Meyers-Levy and Malaviya (1999). His primary criticism is that these models assume that even advertisements that are 'virtually unnoticed' (Ambler, 2000: 304) receive low levels of rational conscious processing by viewers. He further criticizes these models for assuming that advertisements that may be perceived as irrelevant are processed in the same way as those that are considered to have some degree of relevance to the receiver. Both Heath and Ambler suggest that advertising passively builds associations

40

between brand names and attributes. These associations may then influence decision making, but at an intuitive rather than conscious level.

Their views are supported by Ehrenberg (2001), who asserts that competitive products are seen as substitutable and that consumers frequently are not exclusively loyal to one single brand but will usually have repertoires of brands to which they will have split loyalty. In such situations, the role of advertising focuses on:

> reinforcement of existing propensities to buy it as one of several acceptable brands – nudging such consumers to buy it more often.
>
> (Barnard and Ehrenberg, 1997: 22)

Further support for the concept of a weak force theory of advertising's influence is provided by Ambler (2000) who suggest that product preferences are often formed after an initial trial and that, in low involvement purchasing, experience with a product is a stronger influence on future purchasing decisions than is advertising, which they regard as primarily reinforcing existing preferences and helping to defend the consumers' perceptions of a brand. Thus, advertising in mature markets may be substantial but focused on protecting existing market share or obtaining share from other competitors. Failure to maintain presence in the market and awareness among purchasers may result in a loss of market share to competitors. An increase in advertising relative to competitors may result in increased sales, but at competitors' expense, i.e. a zero-sum game (Jung and Seldon, 1995).

Objectives and evaluation

The advertising management process is complex (see Figure 3.2). Effective management starts with clear and measurable objectives. Advertising objectives must be compatible with overall marketing objectives, which themselves must be consistent with overall corporate objectives. These will be substantially different for new brands seeking to grow market share versus mature brands seeking to defend share. Much of the criticism of advertising's failure to demonstrate its effects stems from a lack of the precision and measurability needed for 'good' (effective) objectives. 'To build market share'; 'To maximize awareness' are not satisfactory objectives as they lack quantitative dimensions – they are impossible to measure. 'To build market share from X to Y over the period Z' provides a more realistic base from which mechanisms can be put in place to measure progress towards the achievement of the set objectives.

A further problem with objectives is that they become 'set in stone' and are not revisited if resources or market conditions change. There has been considerable debate, particularly in relation to mature markets, as to whether using

41

sales as an objective is valid or not, given that many other elements of the marketing mix can impact on sales. In addition, there may be a time lag between exposure to advertising and actual sales. There have been numerous attempts to separate the advertising function from actual sales results – to position advertising as more concerned with building long-term brand values than with short-term sales results. This is no excuse for a failure to set specific and measurable objectives (Eagle and Kitchen, 2000).

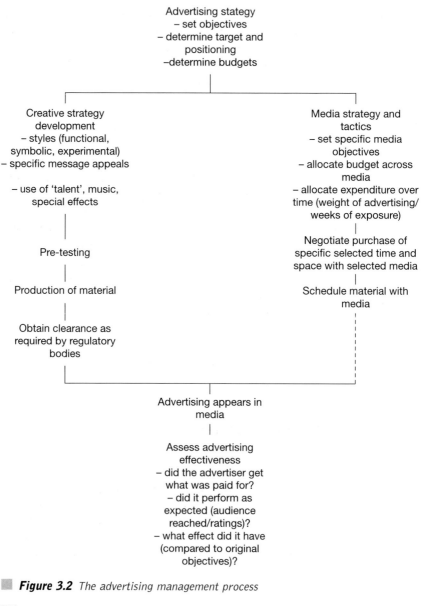

Figure 3.2 *The advertising management process*

There are many techniques for assessing whether an advertisement is likely to communicate the intended message prior to it appearing in the chosen media. Pre-testing can identify an ineffective advertisement, but cannot guarantee success in the marketplace. The biggest, and as yet largely unanswered, challenge for advertisers as the focus moves from advertising as a largely autonomous function to a key part of an integrated communications campaign is how to measure the effects of advertising both as a separable function, and in tandem with other marketing communication tools. While there appears to be widespread acceptance that integration is essential, advertising research techniques have not adapted to enable evaluation of the potential effects and effectiveness of various combinations of communications activity or their synergistic impact (Weilbacher, 2001). This remains one of the major challenges facing not only advertisers, but all sectors of the marketing communications industry.

A further case for advertising

Consider the central role of advertising in promoting special exhibitions such as those regularly staged at art galleries or even purely local exhibitions and displays. Controversial exhibitions such as the sexually explicit photographic works of the late Robert Mapplethorpe may generate considerable publicity, both positive and negative, by their very nature. More 'mainstream' exhibitions such as a world-wide tour of selected works, drawn together from a number of countries and individual art galleries, by the pre-Raphaelite painters will generate no controversy and only low levels of publicity when they reach each country.

Advertising is a central tool in generating maximum awareness of such events and in promoting the scope of the exhibition, highlighting one or more high profile examples of the work on display. Advertising will also feature more mundane aspects such as the venue location, exhibition times and entry prices. It will also be used to keep interest high and to promote 'last days' before the exhibition closes. Consider which combination of media you would use to promote such an exhibition.

SUMMARY AND CONCLUSIONS

Advertising can be a powerful tool within the overall marketing communications mix. It is a dynamic and constantly evolving sector that faces numerous challenges, particularly in terms of accountability in an increasingly competitive world and the evolution of new media forms. As markets become increasingly global and integration of communications activity becomes more sophisticated, new means of evaluating the relative value of advertising's contribution towards overall communications effectiveness must be found.

QUESTIONS

■ How does the move away from mass media influence the role of advertising within the integrated marketing communications mix?

■ What are the major challenges facing advertisers working across national boundaries?

■ How should advertisers respond to the criticisms levelled at advertising?

■ How can the advertising's effectiveness be properly measured?

Chapter 4

Sales Promotion

LEARNING OBJECTIVES

After reading this chapter you will be able to:

- Appreciate the nature of sales promotion and its role in the integrated marketing communications mix
- Understand why sales promotion plays an increasingly important role in the IMC mix
- Recognize the various types, target groups, and objectives of sales promotion
- Understand the different sales promotion techniques, their objectives, advantages, and disadvantages
- Assess how sales promotion works and how its effectiveness can be assessed

KEY TERMS

- Sales promotion types
- Consumer promotions
- Trade promotions
- Sales force promotions

Case study:
HOW TO GET MORE BUSINESS OUT OF GIFT CERTIFICATES

Many restaurants try to promote their business by selling gift certificates. Customers give these certificates as a present to their friends, who can then visit the restaurant and pay with the certificates. Especially around the holiday season gift certificates are good ways to increase sales. Most restaurants that sell gift certificates have a small sign behind the cashiers indicating 'Gift Certificates Available'. The majority of the customers never notice this sign. Since people are overwhelmed with marketing messages – some say over 3,000 per day on average – they block out most of these messages, unless something special is done that draws the attention.

The US restaurant 'Joe's' issued gift certificates over many years. These came in $1 denominations, and were often sold in $5 amounts. The restaurant owner decided to get more out of this promotion by communicating it proactively. He created a small inexpensive coupon, about the size of a $1 bill, which informed his customers of the fact that gift certificates were available for the holiday season. Instead of just leaving these coupons on the counter for customers to pick up, the cashiers handed one to every single customer as they came in. Each customer had to wait for his food order to be prepared, and nearly everyone read the coupon while waiting. The coupon said: 'The perfect gift for the holiday season! Act now to take advantage of this limited time offer: Buy 10 – Get 1 free'. Thanks to the coupon format of the announcement and the special – albeit limited – deal the customers could get, many of them came back to the counter within minutes to purchase a pack of gift certificates. Instead of the traditional $5 amounts, the restaurant sold $10, $20 and even $100 packs. During the promotion period gift certificate sales increased by 415 per cent.

Everyone loves a deal, and communicating a promotion more proactively enabled Joe's to break through the communication clutter effectively.

Based on: Joe and Maria Gracia: Gift Certificate sales leap ahead by 415 per cent, Give to Get Marketing, www.givetogetmarketing.com, accessed 22 November, 2003.

Used with kind permission of Give to Get Marketing.

OVERVIEW

In this chapter, the objectives, target groups, and techniques of sales promotion and their strategic role in integrated marketing communications are discussed. First of all a definition of sales promotion is given, and the strengths and weaknesses of this tool are highlighted. Sales promotion is an increasingly important

IMC instrument. In the second section of this chapter the reasons for this evolution are discussed. Sales promotion is also a category of tools that are used throughout the whole trade channel. Manufacturers use it to stimulate the sales force, resellers, and end-consumers, but resellers also use it to boost their sales. In the third section an overview of the different types, target groups and objectives of sales promotion are discussed. It is fair to say that the diversity in sales promotion techniques used is only limited by the creativity of marketers. Many sales promotion techniques exist, and new ones or new variants are invented every day. The fourth section describes the most commonly used tools and techniques of sales promotion, the objectives that they can help to attain, and their advantages and disadvantages. Finally, in the last section, the effectiveness of sales promotion, and the ways in which it can be assessed, are discussed.

The role of sales promotion in the IMC mix

Sales promotion can be defined as:

> A range of tactical marketing techniques designed within a strategic marketing framework to add value to a product or service in order to achieve specific sales and marketing objectives. This extra value may be of a short-term tactical nature or it may be part of a longer-term franchise-building programme.
>
> (Brassington and Pettitt, 2003)

The word 'tactical' implies that this tool is mainly used to offer buyers or resellers additional value that stimulates them to buy a product 'now' rather than 'later'. It provides additional incentives, such as a price cut on shelf, a product premium, a discount, or a prize, to buy a product immediately. Its main objective is to increase sales in the short run. As such, it is a tool that can be used towards end-users (both companies and individual consumers), but also towards the sales force and members of the trade channel (wholesalers, retailers, etc.). Traditionally, sales promotion has been regarded as the 'little brother' of the marketing mix, a tool that can occasionally be used to boost sales, or as part of a panic reaction when business is slow. However, the role of sales promotion has become increasingly important and has evolved into an important element of the strategic IMC mix. Whereas advertising offers a reason to buy a product, sales promotion gives the customer an incentive to buy it (Kotler, 2003). Sales promotion is a tool that influences the conative (behaviour) component of buying behaviour, whereas tools such as advertising, sponsorship and marketing PR play a greater role in the cognitive and affective components of the buying decision. Furthermore, most sales promotion techniques are capable of reaching specific target groups of customers, and are therefore very instrumental in fine-tuning the marketing effort.

47

In general, the objectives of sales promotion are to generate store traffic, launch new products, boost sales of existing products, reach new customers, increase the usage of a product with existing customers, reward and retain loyal customers, and counter the marketing activities of competitors. Most of these objectives are tactical in nature, and support the other marketing efforts in the short run. However, rewarding loyal customers and developing customer retention programmes is part of the more strategic and long-term customer relationship management in which sales promotion can also play an important role (O'Malley, 1998).

The increasing importance of sales promotion

The importance of sales promotion has increased significantly over the years. Some time ago, advertising accounted for about 60 per cent of the advertising and sales promotion budget. However, over the last years sales promotion has continuously increased its share. Today, it is estimated that between 65 and 75 per cent of the budget is spent on sales promotion (Kotler, 2003; Advertising Age, 2003). This evolution can be attributed to a number of factors. They are summarized in Table 4.1 (Fill, 2002; Kotler, 2003; De Pelsmacker *et al.*, 2004).

Companies are becoming increasingly short-term oriented. Marketing executives are often judged on the basis of the short-term sales evolution of the products and brands for which they are responsible. However, the impact of many communications tools, such as advertising, sponsorship and marketing public relations, only become apparent in the long run. Furthermore, their impact is often only cognitive (e.g. increased brand awareness) or attitudinal (e.g. a better brand image). The inherent characteristic of sales promotion is that its results are immediately visible. Since the objectives of sales promotion are often to increase the number of customers and/or to increase sales (per customer) in the short run, the results of a sales promotion campaign are immediately and exactly measurable. Since marketing managers are increasingly accountable for their

Table 4.1 *Factors leading to the increased use of sales promotion*

- Short-term orientation of marketing managers
- Measurability and accountability
- Perceived lack of effectiveness of advertising
- Brand expansion and proliferation and lack of brand differentiation
- Declining brand loyalty and increasing price-orientation of consumers
- Increasing in-store decision making
- Distribution channel power and the competition for shelf space

communications budgets, they are easily tempted to deploy campaigns that will produce sales results in the short run. The perception of many marketing managers is that it is increasingly difficult to reach customers by means of traditional advertising, because of rising costs, legal constraints, and increasing media clutter. Brand confusion and irritation levels as a result of advertising are high and rising (De Pelsmacker and Van den Bergh, 1998; De Pelsmacker *et al.*, 2004). Sales promotion is often perceived as a tool that is capable of reaching the customer more directly and effectively.

Especially in mature consumer markets, an increasing number of brands and sub-brands are offered. Since the overall quality of the brands has improved, and the functional differences between brands have become less important, consumers increasingly face more difficult multiple-brand buying situations, and shopping convenience falls. Advertising is no longer capable of explaining the difference between brands and to effectively position them. On the contrary, sales promotion offers the consumer a simple reason to buy a product, and makes the buying decision less complex. It reduces the stress that many consumers experience and makes the shopping expedition less time-consuming. Furthermore, consumers become increasingly less brand loyal and more price-conscious, and a lot of buying decisions are taken on the shop floor (Inman and Winer, 1998; POPAI, 1998). Therefore, they can be more easily convinced to switch brands on the basis of an in-store incentive that offers them extra value immediately. Sales promotion is exactly doing that.

Finally, distribution channels such as supermarkets are becoming increasingly powerful. The proliferation of brands, all struggling for exposure, put manufacturers into a position that they increasingly have to encourage retailers to make shelf space available. The retailers, in turn, are faced with a choice of more and more brands, and increasingly demand incentives from manufacturers to allow their brands adequate shelf space and support. This leads to an increasing trade promotion activity (see following paragraph) (Farris and Ailawadi, 1992). Furthermore, manufacturers are also urged to promote their products to the end-consumer to generate as much store traffic as possible, leading to more end-consumer promotion.

Types and target groups of sales promotion

Sales promotion is not only used as an incentive towards end-consumers, but also towards members of the trade channel. In Figure 4.1, the different target groups and types of sales promotion are shown.

Trade promotions are incentives given by manufacturers to members of the distribution channel, such as wholesalers, retailers, brokers, agents, or resellers in general, to help push their products through the marketing channel (Clow and Baack, 2002). The main objective of trade promotions is to establish distribution

49

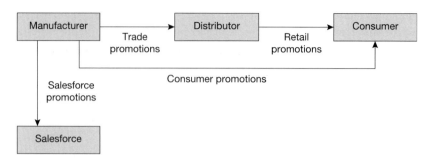

Figure 4.1 *Target groups and types of sales promotion*

of the manufacturers' brands, to develop greater exposure of their brands on the shelves, in other words to stimulate resellers to buy and give maximum exposure to their products, and in that way to encourage product trial and greater usage of the product. Trade promotions such as buying allowances, count-recount allowances, specialty advertising, and slotting fees absorb an increasing part of the sales promotion budget. According to Lucas (1996) and Kasulis (1999) as much as 7 to 10 per cent of the sales revenues received from all branded goods are spent on trade promotions, and the share of trade promotions in the total sales promotion budget is estimated to have grown from less than 40 per cent to more than 50 per cent, and even 60 per cent (Clow and Baack, 2002). In the US, trade promotions account for almost half of the combined advertising and sales promotion budget, while consumer promotions and advertising only account for 25 per cent each (Advertising Age, 2003).

Consumer promotions are incentives given by manufacturers to the consumer, to stimulate them to try a new product, to switch brands, to increase the usage of the brand, or to reward loyal consumers. Tools such as sampling, coupons, price-offs, bonus packs, premiums, and contests and sweepstakes, are used to reinforce the other marketing communications efforts to pull the products through the distribution channel. Although consumer promotions absorb a declining share of the sales promotion budget, they are still used extensively, and take up a large part of marketing communications budgets.

Retailer promotions are the incentives given by retailers to the end-consumer. Similar techniques as in consumer promotions are used (and in fact they are a type of consumer promotion), but the main objective of the retailer is to generate store traffic and to resell the products purchased from the manufacturer.

Sales force promotions are incentives given by manufacturers to stimulate the sales force to sell as many products as possible. Often, incentives such as sales force contests, free training, and sales meetings are part of the techniques used by marketing and sales managers to motivate, assess and reward the sales force. They are part of the overall strategy to push the products through the distribution channel.

From the point of view of the manufacturer, consumer promotions are mainly *pull* instruments: together with advertising, direct marketing, and sponsorship, they directly address the end-consumer to make the brands more attractive and to seduce him or her to buy the product. Trade promotions, sales force promotions, and retailer promotions are mainly *push* instruments. They are part of the efforts made to push products through the trade channel.

Sales promotion techniques

There are a large number of sales promotion techniques and new tools are introduced every day. Often, they are combined with other marketing communications instruments for greater effectiveness (see, for instance, the website of the Institute of Sales Promotions (ISP)). In subsequent overview, a distinction is made between three broad types of promotions, introduced in the previous section: consumer (and retailer) promotions; trade promotions; and sales force promotions. Within each type, a number of specific tools are discussed.

Consumer promotions

Consumer promotions are directed towards end-consumers, and give them incentives to try a product or buy more of a product. Three categories of consumer promotions can be distinguished. Money-based incentives offer immediate or postponed price reductions. Product-based promotions do not focus upon the price mechanism, but use a product to build an incentive. Prize-related promotions focus neither on the price of the product nor on the product itself, but use the chance to win something as an incentive. In Table 4.2 an overview of the most frequently used consumer promotion tools is given, as well as the objectives that can be attained by means of these promotions (Clow and Baack, 2002; Fill, 2002; De Pelsmacker *et al.*, 2004).

Each consumer promotion tool can, to a certain extent, contribute to each of the objectives, but some tools are more appropriate to attain certain objectives than others. For instance, money-based incentives, such as price cuts, cash refunds and coupons, and product-based tools such as sampling and premiums, are most useful to attract new customers, to make customers switch brands, and to increase store traffic. Free mail-ins, saving cards, extra product, and self-liquidators, on the other hand, are more appropriate to increase usage, load up existing users, increase store loyalty, and even out fluctuating sales.

Each technique also has its own advantages and disadvantages. They relate to the consumer benefit, the ease with which this benefit can be obtained, the impact on store image, brand image, and brand loyalty, the manufacturer's and

51

Table 4.2 Consumer promotion tools and objectives

Money-based	Product-based	Prize-based
■ Price-offs	■ Extra product	■ Contests
■ Coupons	■ Samples	■ Sweepstakes
■ Cash refunds	■ Premiums	
■ Saving cards or store cards	■ Free mail-ins and self-liquidators	

Objectives of manufacturer	Objectives of retailer
■ Encourage trial of the product	■ Increase store traffic
■ Attract new customers	■ Increase store loyalty
■ Counter competition	■ Increase own-brand sales
■ Increase usage of the product	■ Even out fluctuating sales
■ Load up existing users (basket filling)	■ Increase frequency and quantity of sales
■ Even out fluctuating sales	

distributor's workload and problems, the impact on the consumer's price perception, the ease of targeting and budget planning, and the immediate increase in sales. The weak and strong points of each technique are discussed hereafter.

Money-based incentives

The advantages of most money-based consumer promotions is that the benefit to the consumer is immediate and easy to obtain, that in many cases they lead to immediate sales increase, and that the workload of manufacturers and retailers to organize the promotion are minimal. Some of these incentives, such as coupons and cash refunds are also easy to target. However, price reductions have the important disadvantage that they can alter the price/quality perception of customers, especially when this tool is extensively and frequently used. The customer is often confronted with an immediate and very visible price cut. After some time he or she may consider the promotional price as the real one, and certainly as the most reasonable one, and new purchases may be delayed until another price reduction comes along (Jones, 1990; Gupta and Cooper, 1992). Another disadvantage is that this promotional tool mainly attracts brand-switching price buyers, and that no brand loyalty is built up at all. On the other hand, if consumers who are already loyal to the brand, buy the brand in promotion, the manufacturer or retailer is just giving away part of their profit without any long-term effect. Furthermore, money-based promotions are hardly seen as innovative and creative, and are therefore less and less capable of having a strong impact. Price reductions always need to lead to a substantial increase in sales to balance the profits lost as a result of the price cut. They are also the promotional tool that potentially has the most devastating effect on the brand image, because the price argument puts every other brand value or positioning in the shade. Therefore, price-based promotion campaigns should essentially be temporary and infrequent. Retailers, on the other hand, tend to like price cuts, because it enhances their reputation of a 'better value for money' outlet, and it increases store traffic.

Price-offs can be organized on-shelf or on-pack. The impact on the customer is similar, but price cuts on shelf are more easily organized in the short run. The price cut for a range of products can be communicated through displays and advertising, and can be easily implemented in the shop. An on-pack price cut takes longer to organize and is less flexible: a certain amount of packaging has to be printed for the offer. Price-offs are often used to launch a new product, and to stimulate trial and brand switching.

Coupons are printed vouchers that the consumer can take to the check-out counter and use to claim a fixed amount of price reduction on a product. Coupons can be distributed in various ways. They are printed in newspapers or magazines, as free-standing inserts (tie-ins), or as part of an advertisement, they are delivered from door to door, in leaflets, through direct mails, at the point of sale, through the Internet, on packs and in packs. In the latter case, they can only be used at the next purchase, and they serve as a loyalty-building tool. On-pack and in-pack coupons are also used to reward loyal customers. Sometimes coupons are issued by retailers at the check-out, to reward customers for buying certain products or spending a certain amount of money. Coupons are used widely and extensively. For instance in the UK, in 2000 about 5 billion coupons were distributed, 10 per cent of which were redeemed (used to buy a product) (NCH Marketing Services, 2001). Reported redemption rates of the 300 billion coupons that are distributed in the US are even as low as 2 per cent (Clow and Baack, 2002). The redemption rate of in-pack and on-pack, direct mail, Internet and in-store coupons is generally much higher than print media coupon distribution, because of better targeting of the coupon distribution, and the fact that mainly loyal or interested consumers are reached. In the US coupons have by far become the most frequently used consumer promotion. Almost 80 per cent of US households use them, and most of them are prepared to switch brands to use them (Bawa and Srinivasan, 1997). Coupons can be used to introduce a new product and stimulate brand switching, or to encourage consumers to buy larger sizes or more expensive products in the product range. They can also be used to make the retailer promote the product more visibly, by giving it more shelf space or putting it in a more prominent place in the shop. Retailers use coupons to promote their own brands, and to enhance store traffic.

Although coupons have similar advantages and disadvantages as direct price cuts, there are some differences. A coupon does not look like a price cut, because the price on the product or on the shelf is not changed. Therefore, the impact on the price/quality perception of the consumer is less prominent. Coupons – certainly those that are mailed or otherwise distributed to a specific segment of consumers – allow a certain amount of selectivity and targeting that a plain price cut on shelf or on pack cannot achieve. On the other hand, coupon campaigns are less easy for manufacturers to organize and for distributors to handle. Furthermore, coupon campaigns often suffer from misredemption, i.e. retailers sometimes accept coupons regardless of whether the consumer has actually bought the correct product. Increasingly, coupons are used by regular buyers (Gardener and Trivedi, 1998), in which case they do not lead to trial or brand switching, as intended, but rather reward loyal customers and reduce profits without any long-term effect. Although coupons are ubiquitous, consumers do not get tired of them.

A *cash refunds* scheme implies that a consumer has to collect a certain number of labels from packaging, and then mail them in to receive cash or a substantial coupon in return. As such, a cash refund is a postponed price reduction, rewarding loyal or frequent buying behaviour. The advantage of this type of promotion is that the price reduction is not direct and less immediately visible, and therefore has less impact on the price perception of the customer. It is often used to stimulate repeat purchasing and to reward loyalty. On the other hand, the benefit for the consumer is less direct, less visible, and less easy to obtain. The consumer has to go through more trouble to get the price cut, and therefore the benefit should be more substantial than in the case of coupons and direct price reductions. On the other hand, since the consumer has to put some effort in obtaining the reward, he or she is likely to be more involved, and to value the offer more. A cash refund is more difficult and more expensive to organize for the manufacturer. On the other hand, useful customer data can be collected (name, address, etc.). Retailers like cash refunds, because they lead to repeat purchases and basket filling, and they are not involved in organizing it.

Very similar to cash refunds are *store cards* or *saving cards*, possibly combined with *trading stamps*. The customer gets a stamp on a saving card (or the purchase is electronically registered) every time he or she buys a certain product. When the card is full (after he or she has bought a certain number of products), he or she gets a discount on the next purchase. Retailers often use saving cards to improve store loyalty and to increase repeat buying. The disadvantage is that they require extra bureaucracy from the retailer and from the consumer. The latter may perceive saving cards as a nuisance (you always forget them at home). Therefore, many shops keep track of the buying behaviour (and the saving cards) of customers themselves. More recently, store cards are used for the same purpose. All products purchased are scanned and stored on a microchip on the store card. The customer of the shop electronically collects saving points that are worth money. The points can be used to get a discount or free products.

Product-based incentives

The main disadvantage of money-based incentives is the danger of altering the price perception of the customer and damaging the brand image. Product-based promotions can avoid this disadvantage. In this type of consumer promotion, the incentive is more directly linked to the product. An extra volume of the product is given for free, a small sample of the product is distributed free of charge, or a present is given when the product is bought. The main advantages of product promotions are that the benefit for the consumer is direct and easy to obtain, the promotion campaign can be easily budgeted, they often lead to an immediate impact on sales, they can be used to both generate trial and increase product usage, and they stimulate store traffic. The main disadvantage is that product-based incentives are often expensive for the manufacturer and can lead to more work and problems for both the manufacturer and the retailer. For instance, for an 'extra volume' campaign, a special package has to be developed, that is some-times more difficult to store for the retailer, and that takes up more shelf space. A product premium (gift) has to be tied to the pack in such a way that it cannot easily be removed, is sometimes difficult to transport and to store, and again takes up extra shelf space.

In an *extra product* campaign, the manufacturer offers more product for the same price. For instance, a pack of cereals contains 20 per cent more than a regular pack and is sold at the same price. This benefit is often clearly demon-strated by altering the design of the pack and indicating the extra volume with a different colour and very visible signage. Another technique is sometimes referred to as BOGOFF (Buy One Get One For Free). The advantage of the latter technique is that it does not require a change in packaging. More product for the same price of course boils down to a price reduction, but is often not perceived as such by the consumer: 'getting something for free' is often a much more powerful signal than 'getting a price reduction', although the monetary value can be the same. Therefore, 'extra product' campaigns may have a less negative impact on the brand image. On the other hand, the amount of extra product should be large enough to be perceived as a real benefit (see also Ong and Ho, 1997). Extra product campaigns can be used for basket filling, or to promote a new product in the product line ('this new product is for free if you buy an existing one from the same product line'). Like other basket-filling promotions, they are also used in 'pre-emptive strike' strategies, to counter the upcoming promotional campaign of a competitor: if the customer has bought large quantities of your product, he will be less inclined to buy a competitor's product that is launched shortly after.

55

Sampling, i.e. distributing a small quantity of a product for free, is often used to launch a new product, or to persuade consumers to switch brands. The consumer can try the product without having to spend money, and may subsequently decide to buy a full pack of it. Furthermore, the unique benefits of the product can be demonstrated on the sample pack. It is the most appropriate way to introduce a new product. Samples are distributed in many ways. They can be available on-pack, distributed through in-store demonstrations, be mailed, or distributed door-to-door. Size permitting, they can even be inserted in magazines, like for instance a scratch-and-sniff sample of perfume. Certain sampling techniques – for instance by means of direct mail – allow careful targeting. And, although sampling is relatively expensive, the budget can be easily managed.

A *premium* is a gift that is inside or on the outside of a pack. Sometimes a premium is detached from the pack and can be obtained at the check-out counter. Premiums are often used to draw the consumer's attention to a product, and to make him or her switch brands or try a product. It is a powerful tool, because consumers like to get things for free. Furthermore, it does not alter the immediate price perception, and therefore it does not harm the brand image (depending upon the quality of the present). The benefit for the consumer is easy to obtain and immediate. If the premium is part of a collection (for instance, a series of cards or toys in a box of cereals), the technique can also be used to stimulate repeat buying. With *free mail-ins* the consumer receives a present in return for proofs of purchase. *Self-liquidators* are very similar, but in this case the consumer has to send money in addition to the proofs of purchase. These two techniques are used to stimulate more usage of the product and repeat buying. The customer may perceive them as less attractive because the benefit is less easy to obtain (see also D'Astous and Jacobs, 2002).

Prize-based incentives

In prize-based promotions, the manufacturer offers very valuable prizes for a limited number of consumers that win the contest or sweepstake. They can be easily budgeted and planned, they can lead to extra sales, and consumers may perceive them as exciting and special, provided their chance of winning a prize is not too limited. In that case, they can improve the image of the brand. A *contest* can be won by demonstrating knowledge or analytical or creative skills, for instance by creating a slogan or being able to answer a number of questions about a product. In a *sweepstake* every entrant has an equal chance to win a prize, based on good luck.

Sometimes supermarket displays and demonstrations are also regarded as promotional tools. However, they are rather instruments of in-store communication. Evidently, they can be used to reinforce the effect of consumer promotions, for instance by drawing the attention to a promotion by means of a display, or by distributing samples during a demonstration in a supermarket.

Trade promotions

Trade promotions are directed towards resellers (wholesalers, retailers), and give them incentives to push the product through the trade channel. In Table 4.3 a number of trade promotion tools and objectives are listed. Whereas consumer promotions are pull instruments, trade promotions are clearly push-orientated. The main objective of the manufacturer is to stimulate the reseller to buy and resell as much of the product as possible, and to stimulate and improve the sales of his own products at the expense of competitors' products, by gaining more product exposure and more reseller promotional effort. To that end, the manufacturer can use a number of incentives (Table 4.3).

In a *buying allowance* scheme, the reseller gets a price reduction for each volume unit (e.g. a case or a carton) sold during a pre-specified period or when he buys a minimum of volume units over a given period of time. For instance, a retailer can get a discount per case of beer if he sells 100,000 cases per year. In order to obtain this benefit, he will promote the beer in his supermarket, in order to be able to sell the minimum number of cases. A *count-recount* scheme is retrospective in that the reseller gets a discount for each volume unit sold during a particular period of time. At the beginning of this period the reseller's stock is counted, and recounted again at the end of the period. A *merchandising allowance* is the equivalent of an 'extra product' scheme: the reseller receives extra volume for each purchase made, for instance one case of beer for each ten cases bought. He can then resell these extra cases. In the example, the merchandising allowance boils down to a 10 per cent rebate. The three techniques mentioned are all price-based. However, they do not lead to the same detrimental effect on the brand image as in the case of consumer price promotions, since trade channel members

Table 4.3 Trade promotion tools and objectives

Trade promotion tools	Trade promotion objectives
■ Buying allowances	■ New product launch
■ Count-recount allowances	■ Improve shelf space
■ Buy back allowances	■ Increase stock levels
■ Merchandise allowances	■ Even out fluctuating sales
■ Specialty advertising	■ Counter competition
■ Advertising allowances	
■ Slotting fees	

consider this form of promotion as a normal way of doing business. Instead, there is the danger of forward buying and diversion by the reseller. Forward buying means that, in a given promotion period, the reseller buys more than he can sell in this period. Diversion means that the reseller buys more than he needs for the area in which the promotion is organized, and ships the rest to other regions where the promotion is not organized in order to sell it there.

Specialty advertising is the equivalent to giving a premium. The reseller is rewarded or stimulated by giving him an item, often imprinted with the brand name and/or the slogan of the promoted brand, such as glassware, desk, or office accessories (staplers, notepads, etc.), or keyrings. The attractiveness of these tools is questionable, and depends on their originality and value.

The manufacturer can also offer to share the cost of the reseller's advertising efforts. This type of promotion is called an *advertising allowance*. The manufacturer can pay a part of the advertising investment of the reseller, provided his product gets a prominent place in this advertising campaign, or they can jointly run a campaign for a specific range of products (cooperative advertising). This type of trade promotion can be very costly, and the effects may be less direct and measurable than other types of trade promotions.

Slotting fees are funds paid to retailers to stock new products (Clow and Baack, 2002). They can be very substantial, and they are quite controversial, because they illustrate the growing power of the trade channel. Retailers justify the slotting fees by means of a number of arguments. They have to invest time and money in a stock of risky products that have never been sold before, and for which they are expected to take other products off the shelves. They also argue that it forces the manufacturers to think and test more carefully before they launch a new product, and that slotting fees help to reduce new product failures. Finally, they perceive the readiness of manufacturers to invest in slotting fees as a commitment and faith in their new product. Manufacturers complain that slotting fees are practically a form of extortion, and that they are a barrier that prevents small or new manufacturers entering the market.

Sales force promotions

Sales force promotions are directed towards sales persons, and give them incentives to push the product with members of the trade channel. Besides sales meetings and free sales training, all kinds of motivating and rewarding schemes can be thought of, the most frequently used of which are contests, resulting in prizes for sales persons who reached a pre-specified sales target.

The effectiveness of sales promotion

Various studies lead to the conclusion that, although sales promotion can lead to increased sales and market share and more customer interest in the short run, they lead to no effects or negative effects in the longer run. But even the short-term effects may not be guaranteed. Jones (1990) refers to this as the double jeopardy of sales promotion. In the short run, sales promotion leads to competitive reactions that often neutralize the promotion effect. Since most of them are price incentives, they often result in reduced profitability without any increase in sales. Furthermore, during a promotion period, consumers often buy large quantities of the product. In subsequent periods this leads to less sales of the product, the so-called post-promotion dip. In the long term, sales promotion can be harmful for the brand image, they hardly change long-term market shares, they reduce profits, and as a result of frequent promotions, consumers are 'educated' to becoming deal-prone and price-sensitive customers (De Pelsmacker *et al.*, 2004).

In any case, sales promotion is most effective when it is integrated in the overall marketing communications effort. For instance, the manufacturer can support his brands by means of advertising in which consumer promotions are highlighted. The effectiveness of trade promotion campaigns can be enhanced by reinforcing them with consumer promotions. Marketing public relations events can be used for the distribution of samples or the organization of contests, and coupons can be inserted in advertisements or direct mailings. Promotion offers, such as discounts and contests, can be put on the company's website, and advertising campaigns can draw attention to the website and the promotion. Customer relationship efforts can be enhanced by linking them to contests, self-liquidators, or other relationship-building and loyalty-rewarding schemes. An effective marketing communications plan is built in such a way that all instruments are consistent with and reinforce one another.

Promotion campaigns can be evaluated by means of a number of measurements and methods. First of all, sales data and information from registered purchases, i.e. consumer or retail panel data, can be analysed. The pre-promotion period can be compared with the promotion period and the post-promotion period, and evolutions in sales, market shares, trial, repeat purchases, increased market penetration, regional differences, etc. can be made. In the case of a coupon campaign, redemption rates can be calculated. Consumer surveys can be used to test to what extent the consumer recalls, likes, and intends to benefit from coupons, extra volume, or premiums, and to measure the effects of the promotion campaign on the brand image and longer-term buying intentions and behaviour. Experiments can be designed to pre-test a number of promotion schemes, by varying the incentive value, the type of incentive, and the distribution and/or advertising media used to find out which types of promotions do the best job. Finally, sales force feedback can give the manufacturer an idea of the impact of trade promotions.

Case study:
PROCTER & GAMBLE UNDERESTIMATES THE CONSUMERS' ATTACHMENT TO COUPONS

Proctor & Gamble makes extensive use of coupons to promote its products. In 1992 the company decided to spend 50 per cent less on couponing, and change its strategy into an EDLP (Every Day Low Prices) approach. Retail prices were dropped by US$2 billion. In January 1996, an 18-month no-coupon test was launched in a part of the state of New York, where 90 per cent of the shoppers were known to use coupons. Almost all other manufacturers, retailers and wholesalers believed that this was a meaningful strategy, and some of them followed P&G's decision. However, the no-coupon strategy met with considerable protest by consumers. They appeared to consider coupons as 'an inalienable right', and consumers in the test region started boycotts, public hearings, and petition drives. Signs saying 'save our coupons' appeared in front gardens, and the local media were bombarded with complaint letters. By the time the protests appeared in the national media, public officials claimed that Procter & Gamble was the company of 'profit and greed' that hurt 'average Joe', and they voted a resolution to ask P&G to abandon its strategy. More than 20,000 people signed a petition against the no-couponing strategy.

After 14 months, in April 1997, P&G stopped its no-coupon test. They agreed to distribute US$4.2 billion worth of coupons that could be redeemed at any supermarket in the region for any consumer or food item. Procter & Gamble still claimed that during the test period consumers received at least an equally good value for money, without the cost and inconvenience of coupons. Nevertheless, during the test period the sales of the company were unsatisfactory. On the contrary, the use of coupons of P&G's competitors in different product categories increased substantially. The P&G experience has shown that promotions are often regarded by the consumer as a normal incentive or reward when buying a company's products. The experience has lead P&G to use new methods of coupon distribution. More and more coupons are made available in more targeted ways: shelf dispensers at the point of sale, in frequent buyer and loyalty programmes, in combination with free samples at the store, through direct mailings, the Internet, or electronically at the check-out. Fewer coupons are distributed through mass media inserts.

Based on: Slater, J. (2001), 'Is couponing an effective promotional strategy? An examination of the Procter & Gamble zero-couponing test', *Journal of Marketing Communications,* 7, 1: 3–10.

🔨 SUMMARY AND CONCLUSION

Sales promotion is an instrument of the integrated marketing communications mix that attempts to seduce the customer to act immediately, i.e. to buy the product now. It can be used to achieve a variety of objectives that are mainly short-term and sales-oriented: stimulate product trial; brand switching; more product usage and store traffic; and counter competitors' actions. Various tools are used towards resellers, salespersons, and end-consumers. Notwithstanding a short-term boost in sales that is often seen as a result of sales promotion, profitable and lasting long-term effects can seldom be noticed. However, as a result of short-term orientedness, the proliferation of brands and products, the need for greater measurability of marketing results and the greater levels of accountability of marketing managers, sales promotions, and especially trade promotions take up an increasingly important part of the IMC budget.

QUESTIONS

- What are the factors that explain the increasing importance of sales promotions in the marketing communications mix?
- Why are trade promotions increasingly important?
- What are the advantages and disadvantages of money-based, product-based, and prize-based consumer promotions?
- Describe the objectives that can be reached by means of the main types of consumer promotions, and their advantages and disadvantages.
- Is sales promotion effective?

Chapter 5

Direct Marketing

LEARNING OBJECTIVES

After reading this chapter you will be able to:

- Appreciate the nature of direct marketing and its role in the integrated marketing communications mix
- Understand why direct marketing plays an increasingly important role in the IMC mix
- Recognize the various types, media, techniques, target groups and objectives of direct marketing
- Assess how direct marketing works and how its effectiveness can be assessed

KEY TERMS

- Direct mail
- Direct response advertising
- Telemarketing
- Mail order

Case study:
THE NSPCC STOPS CRUELTY TO CHILDREN WITH IMC-EMBEDDED DIRECT MAILS

In 1999 the NSPCC (National Society for the Prevention of Cruelty to Children), a UK based non-profit organization founded in 1884 (NSPCC, 2003) launched its 'Full Stop' campaign in the UK to end cruelty to children. At first the aim was to build awareness for the problem and to gain the interest of the public. This was done by means of a television commercial and posters (developed by Saatchi & Saatchi) in which celebrities covered their eyes while sounds of children being abused could be heard. Also in 2000, the organization continued to raise awareness for various types of child abuse by means of a series of television spots with the same campaign theme. In 2001, the campaign entered a new stage. Consumer research indicated that the public reacted very positively to the Full Stop campaign, and that many people desired to do something to help. This feeling was also picked up by companies such as the *The Sun* and Alliance & Leicester. They built a joint cause-related marketing campaign. *The Sun* encouraged their readers to donate foreign currency (unusable after the switch to the euro in many countries) by means of an envelope in the newspaper, and bring it to a branch of A&L. *The Sun* published a daily story on child abuse, and A&L donated £1 per new business contact during the promotion period. This campaign not only resulted in positive feedback and extra business for *The Sun* and A&L, but also in over £1 million donations and 42 consecutive days of free publicity for the NSPCC (BITC, 2003).

Traditionally, awareness building is driven by mass media advertising and continuous media and public relations efforts, while donor fundraising is typically driven by direct marketing campaigns. In 2001, the aim was to integrate the two types of campaign on the basis of a new set of shared campaign messages and creative themes. The purpose of the new campaign was a double one: to stimulate people to contact the NSPCC when they suspected child abuse, and to keep on raising money. Focus group research was conducted to develop a creative theme that would be acceptable and motivating enough for all the stakeholders (policy makers, local authorities, police, donors, etc.). A powerful TV commercial was developed in which child abuse was shown by means of a cartoon. The plan was to build a fundraising mailing campaign on top of the TV commercial that was aired in January–February 2002. This is not an easy task. TV commercials often try to build general awareness. Fundraising is easier when linked to a specific need, and not to a general idea. At the same time, the public expressed growing concern about the amount of money spent by non-profit organizations to promote their cause. The combination of the two types of campaigns would be more powerful if the same visuals could be used, in other words when both the message strategy and the creative strategy are integrated. The NSPCC, together with WWAV Rapp-Collins, decided to design a mailer in which screen shots of the

63

commercial were used, the organization explained the importance of advertising, and called upon people to talk about child abuse and donate money. The mailing was sent to 420,000 regular NSPCC donors and a further 100,000 irregular donors. The cartoon campaign is a typical example of an above-the-line campaign, supported by PR and online back-up (see also www.nspcc.org.uk), reinforced by a direct marketing push. The campaign proved to be quite effective. The number of callers to the NSPCC helpline doubled following the campaign. Tracking studies showed that 81 per cent agreed that the ad made them more willing to seek help if they thought a child was being abused. The campaign had a spontaneous recall score of 47 per cent (32 per cent for the television ad).

The cartoon campaign was the first attempt to integrate an above-the-line awareness campaign and a below-the-line direct marketing donor campaign into one concept with one consistent message strategy and creative execution. The following campaigns will use new creative ideas to keep the message alive and keep things fresh, but will still build on the idea of through-the-line consistency and integrated marketing communications.

Taken from a 2003 D&AD Creativity Works case study written by Meg Carter and used with her permission.

Also based on: www.bitc.org.uk, www.nspcc.org.uk, accessed 22 November, 2003.

OVERVIEW

Due to technological changes, database technology, and changing buying habits, direct marketing, together with e-communications, has probably undergone the most drastic changes of all communication mix instruments. Direct mail, tele-marketing, and direct response advertising have evolved from very traditional low profile and pushy techniques to a potentially highly sophisticated set of tools to build long-term relationships and engage in profitable interactions with customers. In the first section, direct marketing is defined, as well as its objectives, target groups, advantages and disadvantages, and its role in integrated marketing communications is highlighted. The factors and trends that have led to an increased use of these instruments are set out in the second section. An overview of the various media and techniques of direct marketing is found in section three. Section four discusses the effectiveness of direct marketing, and how it can be measured.

The role of direct marketing in the IMC mix

Direct marketing can be defined as:

> An interactive system of personal and intermediary-free dialogue which uses one or more communications media to effect a measurable behavioural

response at any location, forming a basis for creating and further developing an ongoing direct relationship between an organization and each of its customers individually.

(Brassington and Pettitt, 2003, see also
Duncan, 2002; Fill, 2002)

Contrary to instruments like advertising, sponsorship, and sales promotion, which mainly address mass audiences and are not capable of entering in a dialogue with individuals, direct marketing aims at creating one-to-one personalized and therefore persuasive interaction with (potential) customers. In that respect it is similar to personal selling. However, if carefully managed, direct marketing can substitute some of the tasks of the sales force much more cost-efficiently. Due to its direct-to-customer nature, expensive intermediary members of the trade channel are sidelined. The customer can be contacted by means of various media, tools, and techniques (direct response ads, direct mail, teleselling, etc.), but he or she does not necessarily need to go to a shop to respond. Information can be requested or products can be ordered at any location, by telephone, reply card, or via the Internet.

Direct marketing is essentially *transaction-oriented* (Tapp, 2001). It has front-end and back-end operations. The former include communicating with the customer by means of inbound and outbound contacts, making him or her an offer, and to generate a response, usually enquiries and sales. The latter are aimed at fulfilment, i.e. order processing, the actual delivery of the product or service, and customer service functions. One could say that the front end sets expectations and the back end (hopefully) meets them (Duncan, 2002). Consequently, the success of direct marketing campaigns does not only depend upon attractive offers and successful customer contacts, but also on the fulfilment of the promise, i.e. meeting the customers expectations efficiently.

Professionally managed direct marketing relies heavily on databases in which useful customer information is stored and on which well-targeted and individualized marketing communications and customer contact campaigns are based. Although primarily transaction-oriented, direct marketing is therefore also an increasingly important instrument to build and maintain *long-term customer relationships*, by means of contacting individual customers on a permanent basis, or giving them the opportunity to contact their supplier themselves. Contrary to rather cognitively and attitude-oriented long-term tools like advertising and public relations, the effect of direct marketing is easily measurable. Requests for information, sales leads and sales, and response in general as a result of a mail shot or a telemarketing campaign, can be easily tracked on an individual basis. Furthermore, this information can be ploughed back into the customer database to enrich it further and to make it even more useful for future customer contacts.

65

Instruments such as advertising, public relations, and sponsorship, are appropriate to build awareness, carry over information, and form attitudes. Like personal selling and sales promotion, direct marketing is a marketing communications instrument that is most directly geared towards the behavioural stage of the buying process. Most types of sales promotion do not, however, allow the marketer to store the behavioural information, and personal selling is usually far more expensive. Although direct marketing can also be used to contact new potential customers and carry over information to potential and existing customers, its primary objective is to directly influence buying decisions. Trial generation and requests for information are responses that direct marketing is aimed at, but it is at least as powerful in generating re-ordering and in building customer loyalty and customer relationships by means of after-sales service and customer satisfaction management. It can be used as a complementary tool to other marketing communications mix instruments, for instance to generate leads for personal selling, but it can also be used as a sales channel in its own right, or as a strategy to differentiate the brand from its competitors. In the latter case, the brand positions itself as direct-to-customer in all respects, and uses direct marketing as an all-encompassing strategy. Examples are mail order companies and direct sellers such as Dell Computers. Target groups of direct marketing can be possible and probable sales prospects, individuals who made enquiries but did not yet buy anything, former or lost consumers, or existing consumers that the company wants to make more loyal or to whom the company wants to cross-sell other related products.

Direct marketing has a lot of strengths (Table 5.1). Besides personal selling, it is the communication tool that is best suited to build the relationship between the customers and the brand, instead of between the customer and the distributor (Tapp, 2001). Because it is individualized, it can be very persuasive. It allows personalized and interactive communication, and it easily leads to behavioural

Table 5.1 *Strengths and limitations of direct marketing*

Strengths	Limitations
■ Build relationships	■ Cost per prospect can be high
■ Persuasive	■ Clutter ('junk mail')
■ Personalized and interactive	■ Perceived as obtrusive
■ Leads to behavioural response	■ Perceived as pushy
■ Convenient for customer	■ Perceived as incredible
■ Improved service	
■ Flexible and precise targeting	
■ Effects easily and precisely measurable	

response, especially in the marketing of business-to-business and higher involvement consumer products. The customer receives shopping convenience, time utility and satisfaction, and an improved quality and speed of service. When built upon a powerful database, it allows flexible and precise targeting of customer segments and it can therefore avoid waste. Its effect can be easily and precisely measured, and it has a high degree of accountability. A marketer can know the campaign results within hours or days. However, direct marketing also has its limitations (Table 5.1). The cost per prospect reached can be very high, especially if the direct marketing campaign is not well targeted. It increasingly suffers from clutter. People are bombarded with direct mail, and when ill-targeted these messages may easily be perceived as junk mail. Telemarketing campaigns are not liked very much, because they are perceived as unduly obtrusive. Infomercials (television selling) are often viewed as silly and incredible. Finally, direct marketing has the reputation of being pushy and intrusive, due to the sometimes extreme sales orientation of the campaigns.

The increasing importance of direct marketing

Direct marketing is an important instrument of the marketing communications mix. Its use has increased substantially over the years, and so has its relative importance in marketing communications budgets. For instance, direct mail (only one form of direct marketing) in the UK accounted for 11 per cent of total promotional expenditure in 1992, and for 15 per cent in 2000 (Ridgeway, 2000). Direct response television ads (including an action impulse, such as a telephone number to call or a website to visit) in some countries have increased to more than 50 per cent of all television advertising (De Pelsmacker et al., 2004). Within the rest of Europe, direct marketing expenditures become increasingly important. They exceed those of traditional advertising in The Netherlands (117 per cent), whereas in countries like Denmark (almost 80 per cent) and Sweden (almost 50 per cent) they become increasingly important relative to advertising (FEDMA, 2003b). Also, in the US direct marketing is one the fastest-growing communications tools. US companies in 1999 spent $42 billion on direct mail (Duncan, 2002), and almost 6 per cent of all sales are estimated to be direct marketing driven (Direct Marketing Association, 2000).

There are a number of reasons for this increasing role of direct marketing in marketing communications. They are listed in Table 5.2 (Kobs, 2001; Pickton and Broderick, 2001; Duncan, 2002; Brassington and Pettitt, 2003; De Pelsmacker et al., 2004). The collection, storage, analysis, and use of data for marketing communications and customer contact have become increasingly powerful, simple and cost-efficient, due to spectacular improvements in database technology. Telemarketing has benefited substantially from improved call-centre technology to cost-efficiently receive and handle many thousands of phone calls

67

Table 5.2 *Factors explaining the increasing role of direct marketing*

Technology	Market forces	Opportunities
■ Database	■ Changing demographics and lifestyles	■ Increased customer confidence
■ New communications	■ Increasing competition	■ Importance of contact and relationship building
■ Online marketing	■ Media and audience fragmentation	■ More precise targeting
	■ Increasing media and sales costs	■ Cross-selling
	■ Need for short time results and accountability	■ New distribution channels

at the same time. Postal services provide packages that enable companies to exploit the possibilities of mailing as efficiently as possible. Barcode scanning technology has made it possible to efficiently register customer purchases.

Many more people than before (especially women) have a job outside the house. Consequently, families have more income to spend and less time to spend it. Therefore, they are susceptible to convenient and time-saving shopping. This is exactly what direct marketing can offer them. Furthermore, the penetration rates of cell phones, credit cards, and Internet access are constantly rising, and people are increasingly willing to use them as part of their buying and shopping activity. Attracting new customers is increasingly difficult. Competition is steep and brand parity (the similarity of brands) is high. Therefore, the focus shifts towards retaining existing customers, which is not much easier, but certainly more cost-efficient, than having to build business by attracting new customers. Direct marketing is a tool that is particularly suited for building relationships. Advertising media are becoming more and more fragmented. In most countries, in recent years there has been a proliferation of new television and radio channels, niche magazines, and websites. Audiences are more and more scattered over many different media (Stewart, 1996). Consequently, it is increasingly difficult to reach a mass audience by means of a simple media plan. On the contrary, the fact that more targeted media are used by the public, makes it easier to reach a more involved and interested audience, and to aim for a behavioural response through direct marketing techniques. Increased media and sales costs force companies into exploring less expensive and more effective contact methods. Some of the traditional tasks of personal selling like lead generation, sales to smaller customers, or repeat selling of low involvement products are replaced by direct marketing methods. Mass media advertising is expensive and its effects can only be measured in the longer run, and the behavioural response is difficult to assess. The increasing short-term orientation of companies, and the need for quickly measurable results and accountable marketing communication campaigns favours the use of direct marketing at the expense of non-behaviour-oriented mass media tools.

Direct marketing allows companies to build customer confidence and trust. Consumers increasingly buy products on the basis of added value and personal relevance. By means of carefully analysing customer needs, requests, and spending patterns, the direct marketer is capable of addressing specific target groups, can offer more relevant and better-targeted benefits, and can in that way build long-lasting and profitable relationships with loyal customers. The detailed knowledge of the customer's needs and preferences, and a relationship with the customer that is built on confidence and trust, also enables the marketer to cross-sell related products. A well-organized database of loyal customers creates many cross-selling opportunities. Finally, one of the traditional weaknesses of direct selling is the long lead time between the order intake and the fulfilment. Improved logistics and distribution methods have reduced this gap to one or two days, and have created the opportunity of increased customer satisfaction through speedy delivery.

Direct marketing techniques and media

The scope of direct marketing media is wide. It uses traditional mass media channels, such as television and print, but also specific techniques such as direct mail, telemarketing, teleshopping and mail order selling. In Figure 5.1 an overview of direct marketing techniques and media is given. One direct marketing technique that is not mentioned is e-communication and e-selling. This particular category of techniques will be discussed in Chapter 8.

Direct mail

Direct mail is material distributed through the postal system to the (potential) customer at his or her home or business address to promote a product. It can be a letter, a sample, or a catalogue. Most people on the mailing list have not requested the mail, but normally they are selected on the basis of a number of criteria. Direct mail is widely used, especially in business-to-business operations. For instance, in 2001 in the UK, it is estimated to account for more than 12 per cent of promotional expenses (Brassington and Pettitt, 2003). On average, in Europe $86 per person is annually spent on direct mailing, ranging from more than $152 in The Netherlands to $26 in Italy (Singh, 2001). The recipient is made aware of the offer by opening the letter, he or she gets interested in the offer and – if everything goes well – desires to want to learn more about the

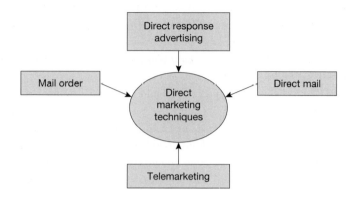

Figure 5.1 *Direct marketing techniques and media*

product or to buy it. The letter also indicates what action should be taken to receive more information or to buy the product, in other words a good direct mail contains a call for action, and efficiently guides people through all the stages of the buying process in one letter. Direct mail has many advantages (Table 5.3). If it is based on a high-quality database, it allows careful targeting of specific customer segments. Mails can also be personalized, which give them a direct-ness and intimacy that most other communications media cannot achieve. It is

Table 5.3 *Advantages and limitations of direct mail and telemarketing*

Direct mail		Telemarketing	
Advantages	Limitations	Advantages	Limitations
■ Careful targeting	■ Bad database	■ Direct interaction	■ Good organization is necessary
	■ Bad selection of mailing list	■ Immediate service and feedback	■ Intrusive
■ Personalization	■ Intrusive	■ Flexible	■ Legal constraints
■ Flexible	■ Low response rates	■ Tailor-made	
■ Creative		■ Cost-efficient	
■ Involving		■ Targeted	
■ Attention-holding	■ Legal constraints	■ Measurable	
■ Measurable effects			

also a flexible medium, because all kinds of things can be sent, from letters to samples and catalogues. The content of the mail can be very creative and involving. Attention-grabbing devices like cards that have to be unfolded or small presents or gimmicks can be included. Even the envelope itself can be inviting and teasing, for instance by means of showing a glimpse of its content through a window in the envelope. However, it is sometimes argued that the envelope should be as unobtrusive as possible to create the impression that it is not advertising but contains an important message. In general, direct mail is also capable of holding the attention – albeit for a brief moment – much better than mass media advertising. It can be used to stimulate inquiries, generate leads, direct people to a website, or sell products. The effect of a direct mail campaign can easily be measured.

A direct mail is only as efficient as the database that was used to compose the mailing list. Lists can be purchased from specialized agencies or internally composed and updated. An internally composed list is usually more expensive, but – if well managed – often contains fewer errors than an externally purchased one. Mailing lists should be regularly updated and cleaned. It is estimated that as much as 37 per cent of business data become incorrect within a year (Miles, 2001). Due to the lack of completeness and detail of databases and less careful selection of mailing lists, many people receive irrelevant or annoying letters. For instance, men receive a promotional letter for pregnancy clothing, or people receive letters for members of the family that have passed away. Therefore, direct mail suffers from a bad reputation. 'Junk mail' is the description used to indicate unsolicited and irrelevant direct mails. In the UK, almost 40 per cent of consumers find direct mail intrusive, and only 70 per cent is opened and 43 per cent read. Response rates are on average 10 per cent, but can be as low as 3 per cent (Brassington and Pettitt, 2003). Marketers can try to avoid these inefficiencies by keeping their databases up to date and detailed, by cleaning the database frequently, and by carefully selecting mailing lists that only contain people that can be expected to be interested in the offer, or that are a member of the target group. Greater sophistication in database management and higher-quality execution can enhance the quality of direct mail campaigns. Direct mail is subject to legal constraints in many European countries. Furthermore, they can be different from one country to another. In some countries people have to opt-in to receive direct mails, or list broking (selling mailing lists to other companies) is not allowed without the prior consent of the individual.

Telemarketing

In Europe, telemarketing accounts for expenditures of over €12 million. They have been steadily increasing over the last decade (FEDMA, 2003b). In telemarketing a direct and verbal interaction with the individuals of the target group is effectuated. It can be inbound or outbound. In outbound calling, the marketer takes the initiative to contact the potential customer, for instance to update a database, to carry out marketing research or for test marketing, to generate or screen sales leads and make appointments for salespersons, or to (cross) sell products. Inbound calls are initiated by someone who wants to make a complaint, ask for inquiries, participate in a contest or any other form of sales promotion, or buy a product. Often these inbound calls are stimulated through direct mailing or direct response advertising. Both inbound and outbound telemarketing can be used as part of a customer care or customer service strategy, by stimulating or enabling customers to complain or make suggestions.

Telemarketing has many advantages. There is a direct interaction and a verbal dialogue with the customer, problems or inquiries can immediately be addressed, and immediate feedback can be given. The interaction is flexible and can be tailor-made. It is a cheap way of maintaining frequent personal contacts with customers. It can also cost-efficiently replace part of the personal selling function, for instance to make appointments, generate repeat purchase, or follow up on leads. Tele-marketing allows highly targeted communications and its effects are highly measurable and accountable.

Telemarketing also has a number of limitations. A call centre has to be well organized to efficiently handle inbound calls. For instance, reactions to a direct response television ad may be massive and instantaneous. Within minutes the call centre should be capable of handling thousands of incoming calls. Outbound tele-marketing is often not very well received by consumers. They often perceive it as very intrusive, especially if the purpose of the call is information gathering or hard selling. However, customers do like to be contacted for customer care reasons, i.e. to check upon their satisfaction with a product or a service, or to thank them for buying one. As in direct mailing, regulatory issues and constraints should be taken into account. For instance, in some countries it is not allowed to call people without their prior consent.

Mail order

Mail order involves the purchase of a product featured in a catalogue. It is a very traditional form of marketing that is also referred to as home shopping. The latter also includes online purchases and teleshopping, but mail order shopping still accounts for the majority of the home shopping purchases. Home shopping has grown rapidly in recent years, in the UK as much as 20 per cent per year (Brassington and also Pettitt, 2003). Besides mail order catalogues, more modern media are also used, such as video tapes and CD-roms. Some companies place the whole catalogue on their website. Sometimes catalogues are sent by shops. In that case, they are not a home shopping medium, but serve as an advertising tool to stimulate people to come to the shop. In non-store catalogues, the customer has to order the product by mail.

Traditional mail order catalogues suffer from a bad image. Often, the quality of the products offered used to be low, and the range of products and deals was often ill-targeted, did not always fit the customers' needs, and was often regarded as irrelevant. Catalogues had the reputation that they were only used to seduce people into buying expensive products that they do not really needed, because of the seemingly attractive customer credit schemes. Delivery of the products was often extremely slow. However, sophisticated database technology allows more careful targeting, and the quality of the products and the speed of delivery have improved substantially.

On the other hand, consumers tend to like catalogues. They are seen as less pushy and more low pressure than direct mailing or telemarketing. People can browse through them at their own leisure and convenience, and they are often seen as interesting and amusing. They save time, and payments can often be delayed. Yet the products cannot be seen, touched or tried, and they are not immediately available. A telephone call and a direct mail have an extremely short lifetime. Once the call is over, or the direct mail is opened, the impact is gone. Catalogues have an impact for a longer period of time. Furthermore, they allow the company to sideline the expensive trade channel. But home delivery requires extensive and efficient back office logistics. Finally, in business-to-business marketing catalogues are often essential and accepted selling tools.

Direct response advertising

Direct response advertising is a message in a traditional mass medium that asks the reader, viewer, or listener to respond directly to the sender to ask for further information or to buy a product. The receivers of the message are invited to send back a coupon (print media), to call a (toll-free) telephone number, or to visit a website. Consequently, the action impulse leads to inbound telemarketing, website visits, and/or coupon redemption. Direct response advertising will only be effective if the offer is relevant and if it is at the core of the message, and if the ordering and delivery mechanism is as easy as possible. Since it is not based on mailing lists or databases, it cannot be as easily focused upon specific customer segments as direct mail or outbound telemarketing. This is certainly true for most direct response television advertising. Nevertheless, DRTV advertising can be very effective. For instance, Directel, a German telecom operator, managed to generate 15,000 calls during a DRTV campaign between June and September 2000, which was 40 per cent more than previous non-DRTV campaigns (FEDMA, 2003a). Inserting direct response ads in specialised magazines or niche radio and television channels allows more fine-tuned targeting. Direct response radio advertising becomes increasingly important, amongst other things because the increasing penetration of mobile phones gives people the opportunity to react to a direct radio ad in the car. However, direct response radio ads are still more effective during off-peak hours than between 7 and 9 a.m. and 4 and 6 p.m. (Verhoef *et al.*, 2000).

Direct response advertising is often aimed at stimulating home shopping or teleshopping. This can be done by means of a standard advertisement in a mass medium, or by means of *infomercials*. The latter is a technique that is used by home shopping television channels. An infomercial is 'programme length advertising' (Evans, 1994). During a television programme that can run as long as 30 minutes, a product is demonstrated, often before a live audience, and viewers are persuaded to order it by telephone. Contrary to traditional advertising spots in which often sophisticated creative techniques are used, infomercials are relatively cheap, because of their simple format. The only things that are needed is a product and a presenter. Infomercials and home shopping channels are not always very successful. People often regard infomercials as incredible and silly, and are not always willing to sit out the whole programme, let alone order the product. As with mail order purchases, the product cannot be tried and is not immediately available after it has been purchased.

The effectiveness of direct marketing

As is evident for all marketing communications tools, the effectiveness of direct marketing is substantially enhanced if it is well integrated into the IMC mix. For instance, direct marketing can be used for lead generation, to feed important information to the sales force to make their sales calls more effective, and to avoid them calling upon 'cold' contacts instead of probable prospects. Direct marketing can be used in combination with sales promotion and advertising campaigns. The resulting information can be integrated in the customer database, and can subsequently be used to analyse which sales promotions worked better than others, and which appeal was most effective. This information can be very useful for strategic advertising planners, advertising creatives and promotion managers. Obviously, the communication strategy and the creative style of all communication campaigns should be consistent and well integrated. Direct marketing can also be used to direct potential customers to a website, or react to in-bound calls as a result of a (direct response) advertising campaign. Different forms of direct marketing can also be combined, for instance a telemarketing campaign can be followed by a better-targeted mail shot. Well-designed databases and direct marketing campaigns are also vital in a fully integrated strategy of customer contact and customer relationship building: handling requests for information and complaints, organizing after-sales service, cross-selling, etc. These database-driven and customer-oriented strategies are more extensively covered in Chapter 9.

Direct marketing is one of the communications tools the effectiveness of which can be most easily and comprehensively measured. On the basis of database information, purchasing trends and differences between the buying behaviour of customer segments and even individual customers can be tracked in detail. When information about the timing and the measured effects of marketing campaigns is also integrated into the database, a range of interesting questions can be answered: do our customers know our selling arguments?; what is the attitude they have towards our brands?; do we see any effect of our latest sales promotion campaign?; which items are they most inclined to buy?; how often do they buy?; how much money do they spend every time they buy something?; how long since they have contacted us?; is our customer base changing and how is it changing?

The effect of specific direct marketing campaigns can be measured quickly and easily. The number of responses relative to the number of direct mails sent (the redemption or response rate), or the number of orders relative to the total response (conversion rate) can be calculated within days or weeks after the campaign. The effectiveness of a telemarketing campaign or a direct response advertisement can be judged in a similar way. The result of a mail order catalogue campaign can be assessed by counting the number of orders, calculating their monetary value, and analysing the customers that placed an order. Before executing a direct marketing campaign, various pre-tests can be performed. In *list testing* the mail is sent to a random subsample of the database that the marketer intends to use. If this test mail produces satisfactory results, the whole list can be mailed with less risk. The *offer made* is one of the most crucial success factors in a direct marketing campaign. If it does not appeal to the target group, the campaign will be largely ineffective. Therefore also the offer should be tested. Similar to advertising campaigns, also the *creative execution* and the copy, for instance of a mail or a direct response ad, can be tested. Contacting customers too often may irritate them, and could lead to the loss of valuable opportunities. Therefore, the *optimal frequency* of direct marketing campaigns for various target groups should also be assessed (Clow and Baack, 2002; Duncan, 2002).

SUMMARY AND CONCLUSION

Direct marketing is an increasingly important instrument of the integrated marketing communications mix. It taps into the increasing need for relevant and value-adding communication. It enables the marketer to interactively and directly communicate with highly targeted consumer segments, even with individual customers on a one-to-one basis, and to send relevant tailor-made messages and directly stimulate purchases. It can avoid

expensive trade channels and cost-efficiently replace personal selling functions. It allows the marketer to engage in long-term relationship building
contacts with his customer and to facilitate customer care and customer
service. Besides an efficient transaction-oriented technique, direct marketing is also an essential building block in customer relationship management.
And although fairly traditional communication media such as direct mail
and teleselling are used, the quality and efficiency of direct marketing
operations have greatly improved because of more powerful database and
communication technology and better database construction, maintenance,
and management.

QUESTIONS

- What is the role of direct marketing in the integrated marketing communications mix and what are its specific strengths?
- What are the objectives and target groups of direct marketing?
- How can direct marketing be used in customer care and customer relationship strategies?
- Why is direct marketing an increasingly important communication technique?
- Compare the advantages and disadvantages of direct mail and telemarketing.
- How can direct marketing be made more effective, and how can its effectiveness be measured ?

Chapter 6

Marketing
Public Relations

LEARNING OBJECTIVES

After reading this chapter you will be able to:

- Appreciate the nature of marketing PR and its role in the integrated marketing communications mix
- Understand how marketing PR differs from conventional public relations and from publicity
- Discuss the main tasks that marketing PR can achieve
- Understand the complexity of setting objectives for marketing PR and appropriate evaluation techniques
- Debate how marketing PR works within an integrated marketing communications mix and discuss the challenges in determining how its effectiveness can be assessed

KEY TERMS

- Publicity
- Public relations
- Marketing PR
- Corporate communications
- Proactive versus reactive

Case study:
THE DEMISE OF PAN-PHARMACEUTICAL

In mid-2003, the suspension, on the grounds of having uncovered evidence of serious product safety and quality breaches (TGA, 2003), of the manufacturing licence of Australasia's largest manufacturer of herbal, vitamin, and nutritional supplements resulted in a series of product recalls: some 1,800 products were withdrawn in Australia and 1,500 in New Zealand, making this by far the largest product recall in Australasian history. The company, Pan-Pharmaceuticals, manufactured not only its own product range, but also contract-manufactured products for a large number of companies under a range of brand names. The bulk of the affected company's activities were based in the Australian market, with the organization supplying 40 per cent of the Australian complementary medicines market, however, 15 per cent of its total sales were in the New Zealand market and smaller quantities of Pan-manufactured stock were available in some 40 countries. The impact of the withdrawal was therefore felt in countries as diverse as Vietnam, the UK, and Canada. The unprecedented scale of the withdrawal across so many brands had the potential for contamination of the reputations not only of the companies whose products were produced by Pan, but also companies who did not use Pan in any way, and impacted on the complementary and alternative medicines category as a whole.

Blackmores, a substantial Australian-headquartered company were not caught directly in the recall as none of their product range was manufactured by Pan. They faced a potential 'contamination-by-default' challenge due to the impact of a considerable amount of negative publicity about the entire complementary and alternative medicines sector. Initial marketing PR activity therefore concentrated on providing reassurance to both retailers and consumers of 'trusted brand' and 'responsible, research-based products' respectively. They also focused significant resources on internal communication to reassure their own staff and a range of other 'publics', suggesting that they were well prepared (they were, in fact, the only company in this sector that appears to have had a crisis plan) and able to leverage 'good relationships with the key stakeholders who we needed to communicate with to manage the situation – including the media, contract manufacturers, retail partners and staff'. They credit the successful outcome for the company as stemming from: strong leadership from the Blackmores CEO that ensured a clear, focused plan and internal communication; immediacy in terms of timely messages to key stakeholders assuring them Blackmores were unaffected; and their willingness to talk to the media when many competitors were refusing. This latter point in fact enabled Blackmores to utilize a considerable amount of free publicity to communicate key messages to all stakeholders. They note that they were in fact doing two tasks. The first was primarily focused on the Blackmores brand position; the second related to ensuring that the messages also reinforced the overall integrity of the industry and the role of complementary healthcare.

While Blackmores ran mass media (newspaper and radio) advertising as part of an integrated communications programme, television was seen as too expensive. They were careful in all forms of communication to 'not slander anyone else' and to ensure that all messages to all stakeholders were consistent. Blackmores also stressed the multi-phased nature of their communication, commencing with a focus on reinforcing consumer confidence and 'defending the safety and efficacy of complementary medicines in the weeks immediately after the recall', then focusing on 'confidence in the brand' and details of 'product solutions' in later weeks. They stress that media chosen had to be suitable for the communication requirements at any given moment and evolving consumer perceptions towards the category and their specific brand, with material altered on the basis of media coverage and of their own tracking research which assessed consumer attitudes throughout the crisis period.

Blackmores also suggest that their integrated, multimedia activity was warranted on the following basis:

- Multimedia approach facilitated the communication of consistent brand messages across a variety of environments and mindsets.
- Print media were essential to the delivery of detail.
- Online to draw customers seeking more information to company website.
- Prominent positioning, speed of response, size and scale of media deployed, all contributed to a brand leadership perception.

Throughout the period, it was deemed essential that only those environments that were consistent with the brand's image were deployed and that a thorough checking of all facts, coupled with a centralized sign-off system was implemented.

These activities enabled Blackmores to rise above the confusion and negative publicity surrounding the product recall. While marketing costs increased significantly in the short term because of the need to ensure that all market sectors and all key stakeholders were reassured that Blackmores were unaffected, sales increased substantially, and the overall impact on profit was positive.

Details reproduced with permission of Blackmores Ltd, Australia.

OVERVIEW

In this chapter, the evolution of Marketing Public Relations (MPR) from its origins within the broader areas of marketing, public relations, publicity functions, and marketing communications are discussed. The strategic orientation of MPR and its role within integrated marketing communications programmes is then reviewed in terms of key activities. The challenges, many of which are common to all other marketing communications activities, of the evaluation of the effectiveness of MPR are then discussed.

Marketing, public relations, publicity, and MPR

The primary purpose of business is to create satisfied customers who continue to buy a firm's products over time. In order to create satisfied customers the company has to provide products that fulfil wants and needs, at prices that are acceptable, available through places or spaces where customers expect to buy, and by effective integrated communication or promotion in order to inform, persuade, and remind target markets and audiences. By definition, marketing is primarily concerned with exchange processes.

However, it would be an extremely poor business that did not extend its relationships beyond customers. The business has to build relations of trust with key publics, constituencies or stakeholders. To create and maintain such relationships, the firm or business requires the discipline of public relations because PR can play an important strategic role in managing organizational relationships with external and internal stakeholder groups whose support may be crucial to organizational success.

Thus, we can see that marketing chiefly focuses on successful exchanges with customers (existent and potential), whereas public relations extends beyond marketing to building and maintaining successful relationships with stakeholders or publics.

In this chapter, let us ask the question again: just what is the relationship between marketing and PR? (see Kitchen, 1997, 1999, 2003; and Kitchen and Schultz, 2001).

- First, it is a contentious topic.
- Second, the relationship between these two crucial communication disciplines is not, and does not have to be, adversarial.
- Third, disputing where the boundaries of each discipline lie, with their accompanying 'turf wars', does not help in settling the debate.
- Fourth, claims over 'control' (i.e. marketing controlling PR or vice versa) are likely to add more flames to the fire.

Our position is rather more straightforward. In order to do business of any kind in today's competitive and turbulent markets, both marketing *and* public relations are needed. As stated earlier, businesses need to interface with, and inform, persuade and remind, target markets, *and simultaneously* communicate with key stakeholders. Put another way, in creating exchanges and building relations of trust, *communication is needed.*

Constant debate as to who 'owns' what discipline within an individual business is a needless waste of money and that even more precious resource, management time. Instead, businesses need to communicate. Whatever discipline helps underpin, augment, supplement, and hone effective communication is advantageous. Thus, in any business, integrated marketing communication skills should be used to help facilitate effective organizational communication. But the obverse is also true. In any business, marketing may need to draw upon public relations skills and practices in order to create satisfactory exchanges. At its very least, marketing public relations – rather than being a contradiction in terms – is seen as drawing upon the skills and practices of both disciplines.

In the communication domain, *public relations* has a much shorter history than advertising, for example, stemming largely from foundations in the early twentieth century (L'Etang, 2002). Its functions and scope have evolved over time, from narrowly defined and largely reactive tasks. Kotler (1980) illustrates the then narrowly defined perception of public relations by limiting public relations to activities designed to sell the organization rather than its products or services, but conceding that publicity, rather than public relations per se, was an element of the marketing communications mix. From the mid-1980s, perception of public relations as more than a tactical device became apparent. For example, contrast the following definitions. From the 1980s:

> Public relations is the process of finding out how a marketer is perceived by its different publics . . . then developing a program to gain the goodwill or support of these publics.
>
> (Berkman and Gilson, 1987: 12)

From more recent times:

> Public relations involves a variety of programs designed to promote or protect a company's image or its individual products.
>
> (Kotler, 2000: 605)

Kotler was in fact one of the earliest advocates of public relations as a strategic tool in his 1986 landmark 'Megamarketing' paper in which he advocated adding 'power' *and* 'public relations' to the conventional four Ps of marketing. Interestingly, his views brought a number of challenges, including Newsom and Carrell (1986) who suggested that Kotler was proposing nothing more than integrated communication! Unfortunately, a number of very recent marketing texts do not provide adequate coverage of public relations in even its broadest sense, and even neglect its potential as a strategic communications tool within the wider marketing communications mix. For example, Perrault and McCarthy (1999) provide a few paragraphs on publicity within IMC – but only two lines on the role of public relations. Its importance as a potential potent marketing communications tool warrants considerably more attention as the decline in prominence of mass media (see Chapter 4) means that effective strategic use of communications tools such as public relations will receive increased focus in the future.

MPR as a specific focus has an even shorter history, evolving largely within the last decade. The change to a marketing emphasis on public relations activity began to emerge focusing on the desirability of the integration of marketing communications activities and the concurrent call for accountability across all aspects of marketing (see Harris, 1993; Schultz and Gronstedt, 1997). Tables 6.1 and 6.2 illustrate the extent of possible public relations functions and the areas in which MPR becomes a specific focus.

The difference between the two is stressed by Shimp (2003: 569) who clearly positions MPR as a specialist subset of public relations, limiting it to an organization's interactions with consumers and stressing its ability to provide highly credible messages at lower expense than advertising. He also separates two functions: proactive MPR as a strategic 'opportunity seeking' function, versus reactive MPR as a primarily defensive problem-solving function, driven by the need for organizations to respond to external influences or pressures. Pickton and Broderick (2001: 490) suggest that Shimp's definition may be too narrow as, while the primary focus is usually consumers, other publics may also be the focus of specific activity. They advocate Harris's (1993b) definition of MPR as:

The process of planning, executing and evaluating programs that encourage purchase and consumer satisfaction through credible communications of information and impressions that identify companies and their products with the needs, wants, concerns and interests of consumers.

Harris expanded this definition somewhat in 1998:

The principle functions of MPR are the communication of credible information, the sponsorship of relevant events and the support of causes that benefit society.

Referring back to the previous section, if there is a gap between marketing and public relations, marketing PR is an attempt to close the gap for the benefit of consumers, business, and society. The term marketing PR is now widely recognized in both communication domains. PR practitioners see it as brand related PR, product support, generalized promotion for products, support for brands through publicity programmes, mainly, but not exclusively, editorial, or PR connected with commercial activities such as trade communications, etc. Meanwhile, marketing practitioners see marketing PR 'contributing to achieve brand communication objectives' and with 'greater involvement in the process of marketing' (Kitchen, 1999). One key buzzword in which marketing and public relations have become ever more intertwined is 'integrated marketing communications' (IMC). Table 6.3 considers how marketing and public relations relate to IMC.

82

Table 6.1 *Audiences for different types of possible public relations activity*

Corporate				Marketing
Internal	*External*			*Marketing*
	Public affairs	*Financial*	*Media*	
Employees	General public	Investors	Television	Suppliers
Families of employees	Local community	Bankers/ financiers	Radio	Distributors
Trade unions	Government/ policy makers	Consultants	Newspapers	Competitors
Shareholders	Trade associations	Stock exchange	Magazines	Wholesalers
	Consumer associations		Trade press	Existing customers
	Pressure groups			Potential customers
				Lapsed customers

Adapted with permission from De Pelsmacker *et al.*, 2004

Thus, both PR and marketing practitioners see benefits in utilizing PR for marketing purposes while recognizing that PR extends beyond the exchange function. As mentioned above, a major driving force towards an increasing inter-relation between marketing and PR, is the emergence and growth of integrated marketing communications (IMC). Does that mean that IMC and MPR are one and the same thing? We would argue against this. IMC is the integration of communication activities, preferably driven by customers and their needs. IMC draws upon any and every communication discipline, as and when needed. Marketing PR is that part of public relations used for marketing purposes. It may or may not relate to integrated communication activities.

Evidently, the boundaries between public relations as a whole and marketing are somewhat blurred. There have been arguments, primarily from advertising agencies that have had the temerity (in the eyes of public relations practitioners) to suggest that advertising agencies coordinate and control all elements of IMC including the strategic direction, if not the implementation of public relations activity (McArthur & Griffin, 1997). This view, unsurprisingly, is not supported by either specialists within non-advertising sectors or, more importantly, client organizations (Schultz and Kitchen, 1997). However, many large communications organizations own, control or have strategic alliances between specialist advertising agencies and public relations organizations. Some even

Table 6.2 *Public relations and marketing PR objectives and tasks*

Corporate				Marketing
Internal	*External*			*Marketing*
	Public affairs	*Financial*	*Media*	
Information	Impact of trends in industry and wider environment	Information	Information (both proactive and reactive)	Support marketing strategy and tactics
Training	Public visibility	Credibility	Opinions	New product launches
Motivating	Information	Trust	Assistance (background material)	Existing product maintenance
Reassuring (in crisis management)	Opinions (maintaining/ improving)	Reassuring (in crisis management)	Corporate image/ leadership	Product relaunch or revitalization
Building corporate identity and pride	Attitudes (maintaining or improving)		Building goodwill	Sponsorship
	Corporate image/ leadership		Responsibility	Special events
	Building goodwill			Community involvement and support, e.g. community fundraising
	Influencing decisions			Reassuring (in crisis management)
	Reassuring (in crisis management)			

Adapted with permission from De Pelsmacker *et al.*, 2004

Table 6.3 *The relationship of marketing and PR to IMC*

Public relations	Marketing
■ Necessity to market the corporate brand	■ Awareness of how communication elements inter-relate
■ Support other disciplines	■ Marketing sets the objectives; MPR is one variable in achieving these
■ Better at dealing with complex messages	■ PR adds value to any marketing investment, activity, or event
■ Not restricted to marketing *persuasion*	■ Media diversity, proliferation of media opportunities are more suited to targeted PR
■ About communicating values	■ Role of PR is still ambiguous, needs also to focus on brands/products, etc.
■ Brand PR an important part of the marketing mix	
■ No need for separate messages when communicating	

have specialist MPR organizations within their organizational structures. For example, the Omnicom Group, the holding company for the BBDO, DDB, and TBWA worldwide advertising agencies, also owns Cone Marketing PR (see http://www.omnicom.group.com and http://wwwconeinc.com).

Pickton and Broderick (2001) review the main arguments in the debate as to whether public relations should be a function of marketing or the reverse and ask whether it actually matters. The truth is: it is irrelevant. Structures and functional relationships are organizationally specific and different organizations have evolved, and will continue to evolve, structures that meet the needs of the organization within the resources available. Thus functional structures and reporting lines will be considerably different in large organizations with specialist expertise compared to small organizations in which broader, more generalist roles are more likely. Further, unlike advertising, public relations is the one communications-oriented area of an organization that may be planned and implemented internally as often as it is likely to be contracted out to a specialist public relations provider.

Whatever the structure, what is important is a close working relationship between marketing and public relations functions, and, indeed, all other communications activities within the organization whether or not they involve external specialists or in-house expertise. While specific roles and boundaries of aspects of marketing communications may be contested, the need for harmonization of activity appears to be supported by all sectors. Gronstedt (1996) argues that close partnerships will foster open communication and facilitate effective joint problem-solving but such partnerships require openness and trust; responsibility for which rests largely with client organizations rather than individual specialist providers. MPR is an extremely rapidly growing area that will continue to evolve and adapt as companies recognize the strategic importance of its input into the IMC mix.

Marketing PR tasks

While the specific tasks required of MPR will be dependent on the overall communications tasks facing any organization at a specific point in time, they will include tasks as diverse as awareness building, as in new product launches, or in repositioning of existing products facing public crises. It may be used on its own, but more commonly it is used in conjunction with other marketing communication elements. MPR's value is in the credibility and/or excitement it can bring to a company or to its specific brands (Figure 6.1).

The case study that opened this chapter is an example of reactive MPR and echoes what has long been held to be the 'gold standard' exemplar of crisis management and of MPR in particular – the actions of Johnson & Johnson in recalling its Tylenol product in response to a cyanide-poisoning crisis in 1982. In Tylenol's case, swift and effective product withdrawal was coupled with full, honest discussion of the company's actions in the media, an unchallenged course of action which, while it cost the company some US$100 million in lost earnings in the short term, allowed the company to rebuild and increase market share in the long term and also 'reinforce the company's reputation for integrity and trustworthiness' (Pearson and Clair, 1998: 61). These examples stress the importance of rapid and honest dealings with all key stakeholders. They should also signal the enormous complexity of managing MPR in the face of a major crisis.

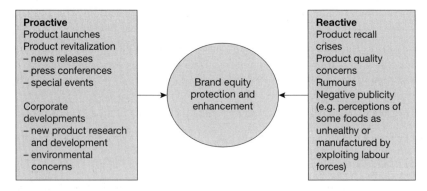

Proactive
Product launches
Product revitalization
– news releases
– press conferences
– special events

Corporate
developments
– new product research
  and development
– environmental
  concerns

Brand equity
protection and
enhancement

Reactive
Product recall
crises
Product quality
concerns
Rumours
Negative publicity
(e.g. perceptions of
some foods as
unhealthy or
manufactured by
exploiting labour
forces)

Figure 6.1 *Examples of proactive versus reactive MPR*

The news media will be quick to highlight deficiencies in information provision, and consumers may perceive relatively minor oversights as considerably more important signals regarding a company's reputation.

There are, unfortunately, numerous examples of how ineffective MPR has actually harmed corporate reputations, such as the 1989 Exxon Valdez oil tanker grounding in Alaska, a major environmental disaster. The company was reluctant to talk to the media, to discuss the magnitude of the problem, or to take responsibility for the environmental damage the resultant oil spillage had caused.

Fortunately, while many texts record examples of MPR in action as a reaction to a crisis, most MPR occurs in considerably less dramatic circumstances. For example, MPR activity around a new product may include information regarding the product being released to the media, retailers, and other stakeholders through a variety of conventional print forms such as press releases, and brochures. Increasingly, audiovisual material is provided to these groups, including to news media outlets, and may be used as part of editorial/news coverage. MPR activity may also extend to staged events as part of product launches, with the intention of not only gaining substantial amounts of media coverage, but also involving and enthusing retailers and internal company staff about the product's potential. Events can be as widely varied as fairs, fashion shows, special exhibits or demonstrations. Whatever is planned, precautions should be taken against activities being hijacked or overshadowed by competitor activity.

This raises the question of commercial sensitivity – being able to plan and execute a particular MPR programme without competitors obtaining sufficient knowledge of the activity to enable them to counter with activity designed to nullify the original planned programme. Marketing texts are full of examples of how advance publicity for special events have enabled competitors to 'ambush' the event by staging a competing event in order to divert attention away to their own brands, often gaining considerable publicity because of their obvious motives in doing so.

MPR activity may also be used as a means of communicating significant company changes or developments or to communicate research and development findings. This latter activity may be intended primarily to enable the company to gain investors who may be willing and financially able to take an innovative product from prototype to full production. Indirect benefits from this type of activity are often overlooked, but include employee confidence and morale. This may result in reduced employee turnover, increased productivity and improved product quality. All these factors, while impacting positively on an organization's ultimate profitability, may be difficult to trace back to the original impact of the MPR activity.

MPR may also be a key tool when an organization is requested, or feels the need, to take a public position on an issue impacting the environment or some key section of the wider community. In this regard, it often overlaps closely with corporate communications functions, which are designed to promote the organization as a whole, both through internal communication to employees and through external communication with a range of stakeholders.

Pickton and Broderick (2001) highlight the success of The Body Shop, which spends minimal amounts of its communications budget on mass media advertising, concentrating instead on sophisticated MPR. They suggest that editorial coverage may actually have up to five times the credibility of advertising, which may go some way to explaining the strong positive associations held by consumers of The Body Shop.

Marketing PR was initially claimed by Harris (1993a) to be effective in at least seven areas. These included successes in: new product introduction (Sony Walkman, Lean Cuisine); promoting mature products and repositioning (i.e. USA peanut marketing); winning consumer trust (banks in USA); celebrating special occasions (i.e. Barbie, Disney characters); sponsoring public services programmes (New York and other city campaigns); sponsoring good causes (i.e. pressure groups in USA); sponsoring sports activities (waste management clean ups).

In all cases, *then*, the outcomes were massive publicity, increased sales, increased brand awareness, brand visibility, positive feedback, and public participation. All these are positive outcomes for marketing and PR. Put another way, as early as 1993, public relations was being used for ostensible marketing purposes and was shown to have something significant to contribute. Note that in many of the successes, the outcomes would have been far more difficult to achieve

Table 6.4 *Marketing PR: purposes/benefits and product/services*

Purposes and benefits	Examples of products and services
Create marketplace excitement	New Volkswagen Beetle, Viagra
Introduce new products before advertising breaks	Advanced Photo systems, Nintendo 64
Bring new high-tech and health-care products to market	Windows 95 (Microsoft), Tagamet MB Ulcer Treatment
Revitalize old brands	Hush Puppies, Aspirin
Maintain market leadership	Chrysler, Pampers
Make advertising news where there is no news	SuperBowl, Sophie Dahl (Opium perfume)
Make promotion news where there is no news	Gillette and major league baseball, Kylie Minogue range of lingerie
Make packaging news where there is no product news	Heinz Ketchup, Doritos, Salt 'n' Shake crisps

Utilized with permission of Kitchen, P.J., 2003

88

(perhaps impossible) if the businesses or organizations concerned had just decided to rely on the traditional tools of marketing communication such as advertising, sales promotion, direct marketing, or personal selling. By 2001, Harris's range of PR usage and benefits for marketing purposes had expanded markedly (see Kitchen and Schultz, 2001; see also Table 6.4).

Furthermore, marketing PR has been shown by Harris to be effective in many other areas, all of which impact on marketing's capacity to create and sustain satisfactory exchanges. These include: building the corporate brand through event marketing (i.e. the Bank of America and its sponsorship of the 2000 Summer Olympics in Sydney, Australia); building a world brand interactively (i.e. Legoland); building a new brand without an advertising campaign (i.e. Star Wars); in the area of social responsibility (i.e. McDonalds Community Involvement Programme); and in crisis management communications (i.e. Johnson & Johnson).

OBJECTIVES AND EVALUATION

As with all other individual elements of marketing communication programmes, MPR objectives must be compatible with overall marketing objectives, and with overall corporate objectives. Like these other areas, MPR suffers from criticism of its failure to provide demonstrable return on investment data. While it may be possible to measure the amount of media time and space achieved by a particular MPR programme, or to document the number of attendees at a particular event, the impact on the image of the brand itself, let alone on actual sales is much harder to determine. Unlike paid media exposure such as advertising, MPR exposure in the media is harder to control – material must be newsworthy to even be considered for inclusion in editorial content. There is a danger of planned activity being eclipsed by coverage of another, unrelated event or high profile crisis.

Often, the urgency with which MPR is required to act, particularly in a reactive rather than proactive situation, means that it is difficult to obtain initial benchmark data against which objectives can be measured. There is also little opportunity to fully test the effectiveness of a proposed activity before it is implemented. The urgency of the situation to be addressed may in itself dictate the vehicles by which MPR communicates with a range of stakeholders. Further, as illustrated by the Blackmores case at the beginning of the chapter, MPR activity may need to constantly adapt to rapidly changing situations.

When proactive rather than reactive MPR is implemented, standard measurements such as recall, awareness, comprehension, or attitude measurements can be used. For example, after a major MPR-originated news story has appeared, recall of the story and its key points (coupled with correct brand identification) could be measured. Changes in attitude towards an organization or a particular product could be measured after MPR activity has run. In common with advertising, there may be a time lag between MPR activity and actual sales.

The challenge discussed in Chapter 4 of how to measure the effects of individual separate communications functions, and their combined effect when viewed in tandem with other marketing communication tools are just as relevant in relation to MPR.

New car launches: an obvious MPR focus

Consider the launch of a new car – not just a cosmetic change to an existing model, but a major innovation in design or performance. While mass media advertising is inevitably a major part of an IMC programme, MPR is always an important factor, starting with car dealers but involving newspaper and magazine motoring writers as well as television and radio news teams.

Invariably also, new cars are extensively displayed in high traffic locations such as shopping malls, with guest appearances by motor racing or rallying personalities. From your own experience, think of the special events that have been organized around the launch – both for the car dealers and for the general public. Consider the 'behind-the-scenes' activity that would have been organized by the car dealers to advise their existing customer base of the new vehicle and to entice potential buyers to showrooms to examine and possibly test-drive it.

Now recall what promotions and events have been staged (particularly if the car's innovative features allowed the opportunity for the features to be highlighted). Almost all potential tools in the IMC mix may have been used here, including the Internet, brochures and pamphlets.

Now consider an area that is very commonly overlooked – namely contingency planning. First, what if you were coordinating such a launch and your main competitor had obtained the details and was endeavouring to upstage your activity. What could/should you do. Second, what would be the worst thing that could go wrong in any launch of this type? Is the company prepared for such an event? What would they do? Who would liaise with the media? What would they say? How would this crisis affect the launch – and the company/brand overall?

SUMMARY AND CONCLUSIONS

MPR is another powerful tool within the overall marketing communications mix. Like other IMC elements, it is a dynamic and constantly evolving sector that faces numerous challenges, particularly in terms of accountability for effectiveness and efficiency in an increasingly competitive world in which new means of communicating will continue to emerge. As for all other communication tools discussed in this text, new means of evaluating the relative value of MPR's contribution towards overall communications effectiveness must be found, particularly as it is likely that MPR will assume even greater importance in IMC campaigns in the future.

QUESTIONS

- How does the role of MPR differ from more conventional views of public relations?
- What techniques are most likely to be appropriate for proactive versus reactive MPR?
- How should MPR be planned and coordinated within an overall integrated marketing communications campaign?
- How can the impact of MPR's effectiveness and efficiency be properly measured?
- How do you explain the emergence and growth of MPR?
- Are the 'turf wars' between marketing and PR effectively resolved by the emergence of MPR? Or, is MPR an oxymoron?
- Review the Tom Harris chapter in Kitchen and Schultz (2001) on MPR. Is Harris overstating the case for MPR? Who owns MPR?

ACKNOWLEDGEMENT

This chapter incorporates some of the earlier work by Kitchen, P.J. (2003) in *Behind the Spin*. We acknowledge our debt to that earlier paper.

Chapter 7

Sponsorship

LEARNING OBJECTIVES

After reading this chapter you will be able to:

- Appreciate the nature of sponsorship and its role in the integrated marketing communications mix
- Understand why sponsorship plays an increasingly important role in the IMC mix
- Recognize the various types, target groups, and objectives of sponsorship
- Understand how to select and manage a sponsorship event and/or cause
- Assess how sponsorship works and how its effectiveness can be assessed

KEY TERMS

- Event sponsorship
- Cause-related sponsorship
- Broadcast sponsorship

Case study:
CAUSE-RELATED SPONSORSHIP AND VALUE MARKETING: LINKING BRAND IMAGES TO GOOD CAUSES

American Express was one of the first companies that recognized the positive effects of value marketing on the brand image. In 1983 the company raised money for the restoration of the Statue of Liberty. American Express donated 1 cent to the Statue of Liberty every time someone used its credit card. The number of new cardholders increased by 45 per cent and card usage by 28 per cent. In April 2001 American Express created the Community Business Programme to help business owners gain access to the resources they need to start or grow. Together with the Association for Enterprise Opportunity and Count-me-in for Women's Economic Independence, American Express helps an underserved group of small businesses and entrepreneurs. The company launched the Community Business Card, a credit card for small business owners, which allocates 1 per cent of all cardholder spending to one of the micro-enterprise development partners. American Express uses this money for entrepreneurs in need of small loans and training. The company has already received recognition from consumers and other stakeholders. As such, the cause-related sponsorship campaigns reinforce American Express's reputation and future business potential.

In October 1999, ConAgra Foods, a US company marketing more than eighty household brands, launched Feeding Children Better, a programme to stop childhood hunger. By cooperating with various anti-hunger organizations, the company was able to bring more food into the charitable food distribution system (using its extensive distribution resources), and put child hunger on the agenda (piggybacking on its promotional and advertising efforts). Fifty Kids Cafes (places where kids can have a decent meal after school) have been funded; fresh food deliveries to relief organizations increased substantially, and some 30 trucks have been purchased for food banks with gifts from ConAgra.

Since 1995 Ford Motor Company have sponsored the Susan G. Komen's Breast Cancer Foundation. The company helps the foundation with donations, media support, and gifts in kind. The company also created the Ford Force, comprised of dealers, employees and the general public. More than 12,000 Ford employees and more than 3,000 dealers have participated in activities of the Ford Force. The results for the Komen's foundation and for Ford have been remarkable. Website visits and toll-free telephones have increased substantially, as well as breast examinations. Ford has been able to create involvement among women, a market segment with traditionally low interest and lack of sympathy for Ford.

Timberland, a lifestyle brand marketing footwear, apparel, and accessories, has been a partner of City Year, a national youth service organization, for over ten years. Timberland has donated more than US$10 million since the beginning of the partnership. The partnership has helped in Timberland's corporate identity building, promoting a service ethic among Timberland employees. They have put in over 170,000 hours of community service. Timberland also opened a City Year office in its headquarters. As a result, the company was voted by its peers as one of the '100 best companies to work for'.

Based on: www.fdncenter.org/learn/faqs/html/cause_marketing.html, www.bsr.org, accessed 22 November, 2003.

OVERVIEW

In the first section of this chapter the role of sponsorship in the integrated marketing communications mix, and its objectives and target groups are discussed. Sponsorship has become an increasingly vital instrument of the marketing communications mix. The factors explaining the growing importance of sponsorship, and some recent sponsorship trends are highlighted in the second section. Three major types of sponsorship can be distinguished: event sponsorship, cause-related sponsorship and broadcast sponsorship. In each of these main types a number of specific sponsorship techniques are used. They are discussed in the third part of this chapter. The success of sponsorship largely depends upon the selection of appropriate sponsorship projects. The criteria on the basis of which projects should be selected and managed and the techniques to evaluate them are discussed in the fourth section.

The role of sponsorship in the IMC mix

Sponsorship can be defined as:

> An investment in cash or kind in an activity, in return for access to the exploitable commercial potential associated with this activity. The company promotes its interests and brands by linking them to a specific and meaningful event or cause. The sponsor also actively markets his association with the sponsored event or cause.
>
> (Meenaghan, 1991; as commented on by
> Cornwell and Maignan, 1998)

A brand of beer sponsors a soccer team, a bank supports an exhibition in a museum, a household appliances manufacturer donates money to a social-profit organization, or a brand of chocolate buys television time to announce a television programme. As long as these resources are spent without any commercial objectives, these activities should be regarded as charitable donations or corporate philanthropy. Commercial sponsorship implies that the sponsoring company has the intention and takes the necessary actions to promote its interests, and to support the sponsored activity by means of integrated marketing communications efforts.

Sponsorship has been defined as advertising, as public relations, and as sales promotions. Indeed, certain types of sponsorship are closely related to public relations, because they mainly support the image of the company as a whole towards a variety of stakeholders. A company that sponsors a soccer team and invites suppliers, customers, shareholders, and other stakeholders to watch the game (corporate hospitality), has in fact integrated its sponsorship project into its PR effort. A brand of soft drinks that sponsors a concert, and uses this opportunity to sample its new brand of juice, has incorporated its sales promotion into its sponsorship efforts. But no doubt the nature and the objectives of marketing-related sponsorship are closer to advertising than to any other marketing communications instrument. The main objectives of sponsorship are similar to those of advertising, i.e. to build brand awareness for new and existing products in the short and the long run, to build and improve the brand or company image, and to reinforce brand familiarity and use. Although sponsorship, just like advertising, can be used to serve short-term goals, like product trial and market penetration, its main strength lies in the long-term support of brand awareness and brand image, and other IMC tools are needed to stimulate buying behaviour in the short run (Hoek *et al.*, 1997).

However, compared to advertising, sponsorship has a number of distinct characteristics, advantages, and disadvantages. Sponsorship can benefit from the strong association with an event, a good cause, or a television programme. Therefore it is a potentially more powerful image builder than advertising, and it can effectively link the brand to a particular market segment. By showing a brand in a high involvement and experiential sponsored context instead of stressing the product characteristics and performance, the impact of the brand communication can be much stronger and much more convincing. The target audience is also exposed to the brand indirectly, i.e. through a third party (the sponsored activity). This can lead to a greater believability of the brand and its claims. Sponsorship is also capable of transcending national and cultural boundaries, for instance by using an internationally known and liked tennis player. Sponsorship is sometimes qualified as a 'cheap alternative to advertising'. This can certainly be the case in terms of the cost of creation and exposure. On the other hand, sponsorship is never going to work if it is not supplemented with and reinforced by other marketing communications efforts. All sponsorship activity requires a marketing support budget that is at least three or four times as large (Clow and Baack, 2002) before it can have an impact. Sponsorship is less flexible than advertising, because it is often less suited to show products, or give information about product characteristics and product usage. There are also some risks that are incurred. A sponsored athlete that behaves badly, or a theatre play that is not a success, may have a negative impact on the sponsor of the event. Some events are overly sponsored, and as a result of this 'sponsorship clutter' and excessive commercialization, individual sponsorship may become less effective. Finally, the effectiveness of sponsorship is very difficult to evaluate.

Specific to sponsorship is the fact that in many cases three types of target groups can be identified (Cornwell and Maignan, 1998). The active participants are directly involved with the sponsor, the event, or the cause (soccer players, employees of the sponsor, etc.). The second target group are those who attend the event (the spectators). The third, and often largest, group are the media followers, i.e. those who are exposed to the event, cause, or programme through media exposure. All of them can be (potential) customers, but also other stake-holders, such as channel members, financial institution managers, employees, and community leaders. The difference between the direct costs and effects and the indirect effects in terms of media followers exposure can be substantial. For instance, Volvo has invested $4 million in tennis prizes, which resulted in 1.7 billion consumer contacts, and in an exposure equivalent to $24 million in advertising (Duncan, 2002).

The increasing importance of sponsorship

Sponsorship is an increasingly important instrument of the communications mix. For instance, in the UK, sponsorship budgets are estimated to have risen from £35 million in 1980 to £800 million in 2000. Half of this amount was spent on sports sponsorship, while in 1980 this was almost 90 per cent (Fill, 2002). In the US, over $8.7 billion is being budgeted annually, two-thirds of which is spent on sports sponsorship (Duncan, 2002). Worldwide sponsorship budgets of $1 billion in 1980 have increased to $16.6 billion in 1996 (Pickton and Broderick, 2001). Between 1984 and 1997 worldwide annual growth rates of sponsorship budgets have been 15 to 20 per cent, and the share of sponsorship in marketing communications budgets has increased to almost 6 per cent (Meenaghan, 1998).

The factors explaining this increasingly important role of sponsorship are summarized here (De Pelsmacker et al., 2004; Pickton and Broderick, 2001):

- Concerns about the effectiveness of mass media advertising.
- Increasing rate of media cost.
- Increased media coverage of events.
- Changing role of governments.
- New sponsorship opportunities.
- Positive attitude change towards sponsorship by senior management.
- Awareness and drive towards integrated marketing communications.
- Relationship orientation between sponsorship participants.
- Positive effects towards various stakeholder groups.
- Need to reach niche audiences and specific target groups.
- Need to develop softer brand associations.

First of all, marketing managers are increasingly critical about the effective-ness of mass media advertising. Mass media advertising clutter, increasing media costs, levels of irritation, and brand confusion all lead to diversification in the communication mix instruments used. Sponsorship is perceived to be less clut-tered, and more credible, involving and impactful than mass media advertising. New sponsorship opportunities emerge, as governments sometimes impose legal restrictions on advertising (for instance, tobacco) and leave their traditional role of sponsors of the arts and culture to the business sector. Senior management increasingly accepts the strategic role of sponsorship in the integrated marketing communications effort. The growing awareness of the need for long-term relationship building between the company and its stakeholders on the one hand, and the sponsor and its sponsored partners on the other, lead to more successful and professionally organized sponsorship associations. Sponsorship is increasingly regarded as an instrument that enables the company to not only foster its relationship with its (potential) customers, but also to develop positive relationships with its other stakeholder groups. Indeed, event or cause-related sponsorship, positions the company as involved, committed, and desirable as a partner, and offers multiple opportunities to tighten the links with suppliers, sales persons, distributors, (future) employees, and other constituencies. Marketing and marketing communications increasingly require fine-tuned targeting. Potential customers can no longer be attracted and retained by 'persuasive hold-ups' using mass media advertising. Carefully approaching niche audiences and specific target groups is now called for. Customers have to be seduced rather than persuaded to adopt a product. Consumer delight and relevant consumer experience are more important than hard-sell arguments and rational product characteristics. Carefully designed sponsorship programmes are capable of reaching specific audiences in an involving and positive emotional atmosphere. They are often much more in line with the modern way of 'consuming' communication and making buying and consuming decisions than some of the more traditional IMC instruments like mass media advertising and sales promotion.

Apart from the increasing investments in sponsorship in general, a number of other trends can be identified. Until recently, tobacco, alcohol, and soft drinks companies mainly used sponsorship. In recent years companies from various types of industries, such as banks, IT-companies, and retailers, are increasingly using this communications instrument. A greater part of the budget is now spent on less traditional sponsorship projects (mainly sports), such as good causes, culture and broadcasting. Sponsorship is also increasingly relationship-based and long-term. Projects aim at establishing long-term relationships with the sponsored organization, and try to integrate the project into customer relationship programmes. Finally, many sponsorship efforts have evolved into global projects (the Olympics, World Cup soccer), with massive global mass media exposure (Meenaghan, 1998).

Types of sponsorship

Three major types of sponsorship can be discerned (Figure 7.1). In *event sponsorship* the company itself (co-)organizes an event or sponsors an event organized by someone else. In *cause-related sponsorship* the company associates itself with and supports a good cause or a social-profit organization. *Broadcast sponsorship* implies

97

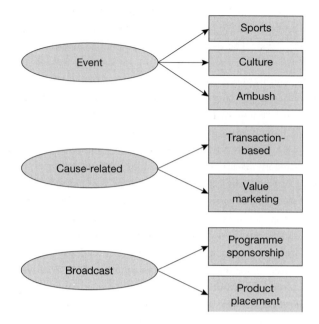

Figure 7.1 Types of sponsorship

that a company formally associates itself with a television programme or uses a television programme to promote its brands. Although traditional forms of sponsorship (sports, entertainment, culture) are still by far the most important, in recent years, cause-related and broadcast sponsorship take up an increasing part of sponsorship budgets (Pickton and Broderick, 2001; Fill, 2002).

Event sponsorship

Events can have a greater positive impact on the brand image than most other IMC instruments (Table 7.1). By associating itself with a sports or cultural event, the company can position its brand in a pleasant and involving atmosphere. It can reach massive audiences or well-targeted segments, and it can link its products to a pleasant experience that is not purely product-related. Companies can create, organize, and sponsor tailor-made events for themselves. For instance, if a fast-food chain opens its thousandth new restaurant in a new country, an event can be created to generate publicity and to involve all customers, potential customers, and other stakeholders worldwide. A company that launches a new product can organize a press event in a nice venue, to generate media attention, salesperson involvement, and customer awareness. This type of event is at the crossroads of public relations and sponsorship, and usually implies the use of many other IMC instruments, such as advertising and direct mailing to announce the event, and sales promotions to reinforce it. Companies can also participate in events that are organized by other organizations, or create its own 'event in the event', for instance by participating in exhibitions or trade fairs.

Finally, the company can also support a soccer team or a cycling team, the Olympics, a pop concert, or a pre-Columbian art exhibition in cash or in kind (for instance, materials, people) in exchange for brand exposure and the association of the brand with the team or the event. There are many ways to associate with an event. Different levels of sponsorship can be defined. The main sponsor(s) often receive the exclusive right to associate with the event as the only one in their industry, they can invite many stakeholders, and get the best seats, they get prominent visibility on stationary, invitations, billboards, and newsletters, and they often have the right to use their association with the event or with the sponsored person (a tennis player or a Formula 1 racing driver) in their own advertising, mailing, and sales promotion. Lower-level sponsors may benefit from only some of these returns. Event sponsorship can lead to substantial increases in brand awareness, and can have a positive effect, not only on the company's image, but also on the attitude towards the company's products. For instance, Heineken sponsored the Rugby World Cup worldwide. More than 80 per cent of all men in the UK were exposed to the Heineken brand name at least 22 times (Brassington and Pettitt, 2003). The European public perceived Euro '96 soccer sponsors as leaders in their industries and as manufacturers of useful and high quality products and services. In most countries consumers felt that they had a more positive opinion about these sponsors, that they were more likely to try one of their products for the first time, and that in general they were more likely to buy the products (Easton and Mackie, 1998). Furthermore, event sponsorship is often combined with corporate hospitality and public relations campaigns, and is therefore capable of building corporate image with both external and internal stakeholders.

Event sponsorship can also lead to negative reactions (Table 7.1), for instance employees who do not understand why so much money is invested in the project, or fans of other teams who do not like the company to sponsor a certain team. Sponsored celebrities or teams can perform or behave badly, with the potential risk that the more negative attitude towards them carries over to the sponsor. Investments in culture or arts sponsorship are generally far less important than sports sponsorship. They are more frequently part of corporate public relations campaigns.

A special type of sponsorship is *ambush* or *parasitic marketing*. In that case, a company deliberately seeks the association with an event without being its official sponsor, to carry over the impression that it is a legitimate sponsor. This can be done by sponsoring the media coverage of the event, by sponsoring one team or one player, or by overstating its involvement in advertising or sales promotion campaigns. For instance, to piggyback on the soccer enthusiasm in

Table 7.1 *Advantages and limitations of event sponsorship*

Advantages	Limitations
■ Positive impact on brand awareness and image	■ Employees oppose sponsorship efforts
■ Involving and experiential atmosphere	■ Employees do not appreciate sponsored event
■ Massive audiences	■ Sponsored individuals or teams behave inappropriately
■ Targeting potential	
■ Corporate hospitality and PR potential	

The Netherlands, and in order not to allow Hyundai the advantage of being the official sponsor of the Euro 2000 European soccer tournament, Hyundai's competitor Daewoo launched an ambush campaign. Against the background of cheering soccer players Daewoo advertised that car buyers would get a discount of €2,000 when buying a new Daewoo car. A judge ruled that this campaign was not a breach of the Euro 2000 'brand name' (Lagae, 2003). Fast food chain Wendy's featured Kristi Yamaguchi, a US skater, in an advertising campaign during the 1992 Winter Olympics. In an impact study, 57 per cent of the respondents incorrectly identified Wendy's as an official sponsor of the Games, while only 37 per cent mentioned McDonalds, the actual Games sponsor (Meenaghan, 1996). In fact one might argue whether ambush marketing is legitimate or unethical. In any case, in recent years, official sponsors devote a lot of attention to prevent ambushers from benefiting from their investment, for instance by demanding exclusiveness both in event sponsorship and broadcast sponsorship of the event.

Cause-related sponsorship

Cause-related sponsorship is often referred to as cause-related marketing, because it usually involves much more than just sponsorship. In its simplest form it implies supporting a good cause or a social-profit organization, like Third World relief organizations or environmental projects. More frequently, the sponsorship is transaction based: a brand promises to donate money to a good cause, a social activity, or a social profit organization every time a consumer buys or uses the brand. For instance, American Express ran a programme in which two cents were given to homeless food kitchens for each credit card transaction by its cardholders (Duncan, 2002). Transaction-based cause-related sponsorship is sometimes called 'sales promotion with a PR spin' (Duncan and Moriarty, 1997).

Indeed, customers are offered a – social – incentive to buy the brand, with the purpose of creating a 'good citizen' image for the brand and the product.

The company can go even further, and become a *value* or *mission marketer*. In value or mission marketing the company defines for itself a socially responsible mission and a set of ethical values, and selects sponsorship projects that are in line with this mission and value set (Duncan, 2002; De Pelsmacker *et al.*, 2004). However, value marketing is more than just selecting appropriate sponsorship programmes. To be successful the mission should be reflected in everything the company does, and in the way in which it behaves towards customers, suppliers, distributors, and all other stakeholders. The Body Shop is an example of a value marketer. The company commits itself not to test their cosmetic products on animals, to adhere to fair trade practices, and to use recycled, recyclable, and refillable recipients. Furthermore, part of the company's profits and of the profits of each subsidiary is invested in social causes. Another example is the long-term relation between Timberland, a lifestyle brand that sells footwear, apparel, and accessories, and City Year, a US youth service organization. Timberland has already donated more than $10 million in grants and in-kind gifts, and has co-organized several programmes and events. As a result, Timberland was voted by its peers as one of the best companies to work for (BSR, 2003).

If implemented in a credible way, cause-related marketing or sponsorship can have very positive effects. Studies indicate that as many as two consumers in three are willing to take a company's relationship with good causes into account when making a purchase. Furthermore, most employees like to work for good-cause-conscious companies. However, companies engaging in cause-related marketing communication projects should respect a number of important principles, such as integrity, transparency, sincerity, mutual respect, and mutual benefit. If not, the whole initiative may backfire, and the company and its brands will develop a reputation of opportunism and insincerity (BSR, 2003). In any case, there are signs that the public is increasingly sensitive to ethical issues, and that sincere cause-related marketing efforts are a good way to create a positive image for the company and its products (De Pelsmacker *et al.*, 2003). Cause-related marketing is an increasingly important form of sponsorship. It already accounts for almost 10 per cent of sponsorship budgets in the US (Pickton and Broderick, 2001).

Broadcast sponsorship

The most obvious form of broadcast sponsorship is programme sponsorship or bill boarding: a brand announces a programme, for instance 'Coronation Street is offered to you by Cadbury's'. This type of sponsorship is closest to advertising, the only difference being that a closer link is established between the programme and the brand. But programme sponsorship can imply a lot more.

Sometimes the association between the programme and the sponsor involves being able to use famous actors to endorse the product in advertising campaigns. The sponsored brand or product category can also be mentioned during the programme, for instance if the live audience in the studio is asked to switch off their cell phones (referring to a mobile phone manufacturer who sponsors the programme). This is called inscript sponsoring. The company can also sponsor prizes in a quiz programme, or develop the programme in close cooperation with the television channel, for instance a tour operator that co-develops a travel programme (Floor and van Raaij, 2002).

Product placement is defined as the use of a product or a product's name within a programme, paid for by the marketer of the product, either by paying the television channel or film producer, or by providing the product itself. Although television channels in many European countries frown upon this form of cooperation, it is increasingly used. In fact, controlling movie budgets would often be very difficult without product placements. For instance, in the Bond movie *Die Another Day*, twenty brands (amongst which Aston Martin, Revlon, Swatch, Sony, Samsonite, and British Airways) are promoted by means of product placement, with a combined value of these contracts of €45 million (*De Morgen*, 2002). Product placement can be very effective, since the product is shown while it is being used in highly involving situations, and by famous and credible endorsers. Studies show that this type of sponsorship leads to increased brand salience, especially when people like the programme or the movie, and when they are not very familiar with the promoted brand (Johnstone and Dodd, 2000).

The effectiveness of sponsorship

Sponsorship can be a powerful awareness and image builder with both potential customers and various other stakeholder groups. It enables the company to create a link between the brand and the target groups in an involving and experiential way. The effectiveness of sponsorship projects depends on how well the projects are selected and how well they are integrated in the marketing communications mix. A checklist for sponsorship project selection is given here (Shimp, 2000; Duncan, 2002; De Pelsmacker *et al.*, 2004).

- Strategic fit between company and sponsorship project.
- Quality level of event.
- Link with target audiences.
- Brand image reinforcement.
- Originality.
- Budgets.
- Marketing communications spin-off and integration in the IMC mix.
- Track results.

The most important starting point is that the company should select sponsorship programmes that have a close strategic fit with the company's mission and strategic objectives. Ideally, the sponsorship programme should allow the company to establish a credible long-term relationship with the project, to consistently associate its (brand) name with the project, and to carry over this quality-level link to its target groups, both (potential) customers and other stakeholders. The sponsorship programme should create the opportunity for long-lasting brand reinforcement and support. Sponsorship programmes should also be original. If a company is merely one of the many sponsors in a cluttered event, the project will not be a success. A certain level of exclusiveness should therefore be negotiated, and the company should protect itself against ambushing. If the company is only sponsoring an event because one of its competitors does or has done the same, it will create for itself a weak 'me-too' image. Sponsors should look for original, difficult to imitate and creative sponsorship projects. As with all marketing communication campaigns, budgets should be carefully considered. In the case of sponsorship, the company has to realize that an effective sponsorship support budget may be much larger than the amount of sponsorship itself.

One of the most important characteristics of a good sponsorship project is that it provides ample opportunities for marketing communications spin-off, and that indeed the company is using them. Sponsorship is probably one of the marketing communications tools that require most support from other tools to be effective. The company should make sure that its name or its brands are consistently mentioned in the communications of the sponsored event itself, that a maximum of media coverage is ensured, and that the company is given the opportunity to extend its sponsorship efforts to other marketing communication campaigns, such as advertising, PR and sales promotion. It should actively integrate its sponsorship efforts into the rest of the IMC mix, by using or cross-promoting the sponsored team, persons or events in advertising, create sales promotion opportunities, use the sponsorship in personal or direct communication campaigns, and in PR efforts, for instance, by means of corporate hospitality.

Wherever possible, the company should attempt to measure the results and the effectiveness of its sponsorship efforts, and involve the sponsored organization. Sponsorship is probably one of the instruments of the marketing mix the results of which are the most difficult to measure. One of the reasons is the essentially long-term effect of many sponsorship projects. It is not so easy to measure the impact of sponsorship on brand awareness, brand image and brand loyalty. Furthermore, sponsorship is often integrated into other instruments of the marketing mix, as a result of which its contribution to the result of the IMC efforts is hard to measure. For instance, what is the effect of corporate hospitality on company profits? Nevertheless, attempts should be made to measure sponsorship effects. Essentially, four methods can be used (De Pelsmacker *et al.*,

2004). First of all, the *exposure* of the target groups to the sponsor's brand can be measured, for instance, by means of registering the number of times the sponsor's brand has been exposed to the number of members of the target groups. Second, the *communication effects* of the sponsorship campaign can be measured: how many people are aware of the brand before and after the event, how did the image of the brand name evolve, how many people can correctly attribute a sponsor to an event, and so on. *Feedback of participating groups* can be sought, for instance by interviewing participants to an event or people who where invited to corporate hospitality events. Finally, the evolution of *sales and market shares* can be monitored to assess the effectiveness of the sponsorship project.

Case study:
DRINKING WESTMALLE TRAPPIST AND HAVING A SPONSORED WALK

The Trappist Abbey in Westmalle (Belgium) has existed since 1794. The dark ('dubbel') and blonde ('tripel') Westmalle Trappist beer is brewed within the walls of the Abbey, under the supervision of the monks and based on traditional recipes. Therefore it is one of only six beers in the world that can use the legally protected 'Trappist' label. In recent years, 'abbey beers' have become increasingly popular. Large companies such as Interbrew have discovered this attractive and growing market segment, and heavily promote their own version of 'abbey beers' (for instance Leffe), using massive advertising and promotion campaigns, sponsorship, and in-pub communications. And although these brands cannot use the 'Trappist' label, in the mind of consumers they are to a certain extent all related to abbeys and monks, and benefit from the reputation of being a traditional and special beer that is usually attributed to abbey-related appeals.

Westmalle Trappist is a small brewery with a number of important principles. The company attaches a lot of importance to durable production and sensible consumption of beer. It is dedicated to using only natural and top-quality ingredients, it does not wish to change its original taste (rather bitter, and certainly not as sweet as many young people would want). It wants to create a safe and healthy work environment for its employees, and tries to ensure that the production is as environmentally friendly as possible. It does not want to focus on young people (Westmalle is for adults who know how to enjoy beer), and it refrains from aggressive promotions. The brand never advertises in mass media, and uses neither sales promotions nor price cuts. The only communication tools it employs are in-store and in-pub communications.

Westmalle Trappist also sponsors a large number of events, most of them established for a number of years. One of these sponsored projects is hiking clubs. In flat Belgium, hiking is a hobby for mainly middle-aged people who love the outdoors.

As such they fit nicely with Westmalle's target group and desired brand image. The company sponsors the clubs in cash and in kind, and in return the brand appears on membership and hiking cards, and is sold in pubs along the hiking tracks. In 2003 the brewery decided to measure the effectiveness of its sponsorship. The results showed that Westmalle Trappist had 80 per cent brand awareness, much higher than any other abbey beer. Forty per cent of the respondents came to know Westmalle during or after a hiking trip. The beer is associated with feeling, tradition, enjoyment, cosiness, quality, health, and natural ingredients, and is perceived as fundamentally different from other beers of its type. Almost 95 per cent of the sample drinks Westmalle at least once in a while. Most people could imagine drinking Westmalle on many different occasions. However, most members of hiking clubs were not aware of the fact that Westmalle Trappist sponsored their club. It seems that the company's sponsorship does not make an immediate and clear impression at the event itself, but rather influences brand awareness, brand attitude, and trial indirectly.

Based on case study material collected by students of the University of Antwerp.

SUMMARY AND CONCLUSION

Sponsorship can be a powerful tool to create and support brand awareness, to enhance brand image, and to build and support customer loyalty. It can also be used to build relationships with various internal and external stakeholder groups. Sponsorship is an element of the IMC mix that has become increasingly important and professional. In order to be effective, sponsorship projects should be carefully selected and managed and should, even more than other communications tools, be effectively integrated into the IMC mix. The strategic fit between the sponsored event or cause and the company's objectives and target groups, and the promotional spin-off potential of the project are very important considerations. Three main types of sponsorship exist. The oldest, and still most important, is event sponsorship, in which sports sponsorships play an important role. But cause-related and broadcast sponsorship have become increasingly important. In their effort to respond to more ethical consumer behaviour, companies pay more attention to their corporate social responsibility, and the growing power of the mass media leads to more focus on broadcast or broadcast-supported sponsorship.

QUESTIONS

■ Why is sponsorship an increasingly important instrument of the integrated marketing communications mix?

■ What are the advantages and disadvantages of sponsorship, and what are the marketing communication objectives it can best be used for?

■ Why are broadcast and cause-related sponsorship increasingly attractive for companies?

■ What determines the effectiveness of sponsorship projects?

Chapter 8

e-communications

LEARNING OBJECTIVES

After reading this chapter you will be able to:

- Have an overview of new media and their growing importance
- Appreciate the nature of e-communications and their role in the integrated marketing communications mix
- Recognize the various types, media, techniques, target groups and objectives of e-communications
- Assess how e-communications work and how their effectiveness can be measured

KEY TERMS

- New media
- Cyber marketing
- Internet communications
- Mobile marketing
- Interactive television marketing

Case study:
ANCHORVILLE: BOOSTING ANCHOR MILK SALES BY BUILDING AN INTERNET COMMUNITY FOR KIDS

Historically, like in most other countries, the milk category and milk market in New Zealand has been a fairly stable and uneventful market. The milk market has been declining for decades, due to the growing popularity of soft drinks, more focus on healthy low-fat diets, and more and more people skipping breakfast. Although each of the three major milk brands, Anchor, Tararua, and Meadowfresh, had a strong position on its own part of the New Zealand territory, this situation was rapidly changing. House brands (private labels) have managed to build a market share of almost 50 per cent in 6 years, and regional brands have developed to become national brands. The upper North Island, the traditional homeland of Anchor, is aggressively entered by the other two major brands. One of the conventions in the milk category is that mothers are the primary target group of milk advertising campaigns. They are the ones that buy milk, and they regard milk as an important part of their children's diet: milk builds strong and healthy kids. However, mothers are quite indifferent about milk brands. Milk is milk, no matter what bottle it is sold in and what its brand name is. The strategic challenge was to elevate Anchor beyond its commodity status.

Research shows that children under the age of 10 represent 19 per cent of the population, but account for 24 per cent of the total milk volume consumed. Furthermore, mothers do not mind being pestered to purchase milk, because 'it beats buying more Coke'. Saatchi & Saatchi, the Anchor advertising agency, decided to shift its attention from mothers to children: the consumer (kids 6–15 years of age) became the primary target group of the campaign, while the purchaser (mothers, household shoppers) became a secondary target group. The creative strategy focused upon a combination of a rational and an emotional appeal, and the brand essence was defined as 'Building bodies made fun'. The creative challenge was to make New Zealand kids believe that Anchor Milk is the fun way to build bodies. The creative execution used Anchorville, a mythical town fuelled by Anchor Milk. The campaign featured characters that were used on bottles, dairies, and trucks and in advertising campaigns.

The Internet plays a very important role in the campaign. Anchorville.co.nz is an online community for kids, and runs on Anchorville points. Points are earned by entering the unique codes on the back label of Anchor bottles. The objective was to become the most popular website for New Zealand kids, to achieve 10,000 'citizens' (visitor registrations) after 3 months, and to achieve a product code redemption rate of 30 per cent. An online banner campaign was used to capture kids online and direct them to the Anchorville site. Four online advertisements were created to bring the Anchorville concept to life. They were used on high traffic and key kids Internet sites. Furthermore, three television commercials were developed to introduce the Anchorville

108

concept, one of which was directly aimed at code redemption and at driving traffic to the website. Outdoor advertising supported the television campaign.

The campaign was highly successful. The brand increased its market share from 6.9 per cent to 7.3 per cent in the lower North Island, and from 8.1 per cent to 8.7 per cent in the South Island. Preference for the Anchor brand increased from 47 per cent to 60 per cent, and spontaneous brand awareness climbed from 61 per cent to 68 per cent in the southern North Island, and from 70 per cent to 83 per cent in the South Island. Correct brand registration was 88 per cent, compared to 62 per cent for the competitors. Pester power through kids worked: on average 34 per cent of kids asked their parents for Anchor Milk, and 70 per cent of these parents actually bought the brand. The online banner campaign was successful: over 8,000 people were captured via banners on popular kids sites. The average click-through rate on What Now, Squirt, and Kidzone was 4.82 per cent, compared with an industry benchmark of less than 0.5 per cent. Anchorville.co.nz evolved into New Zealand's number one food and beverage site during the campaign, although after the campaign Coca Cola took over the lead. Within the first 4 weeks, the target of 10,000 citizens was achieved. After 2 months the site had 20,000 registrations. In June 2003 Anchorville had 37,000 citizens. Of all registered visitors, 58 per cent entered product codes from Anchor bottles. Anchor succeeded in combining traditional- and cyber-marketing communications to revive the brand with its young consumers.

Based on: Communication Agencies Association of New Zealand: 'New Zealand Dairy Foods – Anchorville', 2003 Effie Award case study, www.caanz.co.nz

Used with kind permission of the CAANZ.

OVERVIEW

During the last decade a number of technological evolutions have led to a revolutionary change in the scope and use of what have been called 'new media'. The growing sophistication of Internet technology and the spectacular increase in the penetration and use of the Internet, and the revolution in telecom technology and the use of mobile phones, are the two most striking examples. But also an emerging technology like digital interactive television holds in it the promise of fundamental changes in people's media use. All these evolutions are challenges for the marketing communications manager who can benefit from integrating these new media in his marketing communication strategies, but who will also have to cope with the typical characteristics, opportunities, and pitfalls of these new media and the way in which potential customers use them. The first section of this chapter gives a brief overview of what exactly new media and e-communications mean. In the second section, the growing importance and use of the new media is illustrated. In the third section, the role of

109

e-communications in the IMC mix is discussed, with special focus on the role, the potential, the strengths and the weaknesses of Internet communications. The fourth section highlights a number of specific techniques and media of e-communications, and focuses on Internet communications, mobile marketing and interactive television. In the last section, the effectiveness of e-communications and how to assess it is discussed.

e-communications and new media

In marketing communications the word 'media' has traditionally been used to indicate the classical mass media. The term 'new media' suggests all forms of new media development, but is mostly associated with electronic media. Moreover, most of these 'new media' have been around for some time now, but it is only recently that technological evolutions and changing consumer behaviour patterns in media usage have led to a boom in electronic media use. The most striking examples of new media are the Internet and mobile telecommunication technology, and to a lesser extent digital television, but in a broader sense also CD-ROM and DVD could be regarded as new media. The common and most important characteristic of these media is the fact that they are truly interactive. *Interactivity* means that it is the receiver (the viewer, caller, etc.) who decides what to see and when to see it, or not, in other words to control the communication flow. When surfing the Web, you can read a banner or not, click-through to another website or not, read the pages as long or as briefly as you want. You can opt-in for mobile phone marketing activities or not, and you can choose to watch anything you like for as long as you like on interactive television. This is radically different from most other communication channels and media, in which the sender is at the steering wheel. A second important feature of the new media is their *multimedia nature*. Different formats such as text, pictures, movies, animations, music, video, and narrative, are combined in one single medium. *Cyber marketing* is the term used to describe the use of computers and telecommunications in marketing (Keeler, 1995). It includes Internet marketing, mobile marketing, and interactive television marketing:

> E-communications is using the Internet, mobile phones, interactive television, and other electronic media in marketing communication campaigns.

The Internet is a system of interrelated networks that spans the globe and that allows users with the appropriate computer hardware and software to communicate and to share and exchange information with each other. The Internet is a unique and independent medium, not owned or operated by any single commercial or governmental body. Although the Internet is also used for e-mail applications and file transfer, it is often used as a synonym for the World Wide

Web (WWW), the interactive and graphical communication medium using hypertext mark-up language (HTML) that allows multimedia documents to be shared by different users. The hyperlinks on web pages make it possible to navigate quickly through documents and pages with a simple mouse click. Internet marketing (communications) refers to the use of the Internet for marketing (communications) purposes. Mobile marketing or wireless advertising are communication activities that use mobile devices (like cell phones) to promote products and services. Interactive (digital) television (iTV) gives viewers the ability to interact with the programmes and to themselves select the content they want to watch. iTV communications refers to all communications activity that uses the interactive possibilities of this new technology.

The growing importance of new media

In recent years, the penetration and use of new media, especially the Internet and mobile phones, has exploded. In March 2003 more than 30 million domain names (an indication of the number of websites) were registered worldwide, and more than 650 million people, including 200 million in Europe, were connected to the Internet (Sotd, 2003). Online household penetration in Europe in 2003 ranges from around 20 per cent in Greece and Portugal to more than 60 per cent in Sweden and Denmark. This penetration is predicted to increase to, on average, more than 50 per cent by 2006. However, less than half of the online users actually use the Internet to buy products, ranging from 20 per cent in Belgium to 40 per cent in the UK. The amount of money spent online is rising, and currently ranges from about $200 per buyer per year in Greece to $700 in the UK (Euromonitor, 2002). Already in 1999 businesses placed orders via the Internet totalling $1.3 trillion worldwide, and in the US 25 per cent of all business-to-business purchases are made via the Internet (Clow and Baack, 2002).

Similarly, the use of e-mails has skyrocketed. Globally 500 million e-mail users send around 4 billion e-mails daily (De Pelsmacker et al., 2004). In the UK, for instance, each e-mail box owner receives on average 39 e-mails per day, and twice as many e-mails are sent than letters (Dwek, 2002). In the US there are 200 million e-mail boxes and 7 trillion e-mails are sent each year. Nearly 50 per cent of the US population communicates via e-mail and receives on average 37 e-mails per day (Clow and Baack, 2002).

Also the use of wireless telecommunications has evolved remarkably over the last years. By the end of 2002 there were 850 million mobile phone users worldwide. The average penetration rate in Europe is 80 per cent. More than 90 per cent of the mobile phone owners between the ages of 15 and 44 use SMS (short message service), and the average amount of SMS messages sent per month has increased from 44 in 2000 to 56 in 2002 (Huberland, 2003). In most European countries digital television is not (widely) available or is still in its infancy.

111

The exception is the UK where nearly 8 million homes already have access to it (Brassington and Pettitt, 2003).

The role of e-communications in the IMC mix

Although Internet communications still represent a minor part of advertising budgets, its share is rapidly growing. Across Europe, in 2002, 1.3 per cent of media advertising investments have been spent on the Internet, ranging from less than 0.5 per cent in Italy and Portugal, to 2.5 per cent in Norway and 5 per cent in Sweden. In that same year, total advertising investments increased by 2 per cent, but Internet advertising growth was at least ten times that much. The total European budget spent on Internet advertising is estimated to be close to €800 million (De Pelsmacker *et al.*, 2004). In the US it is estimated that, in 2004, 10 per cent of business-to-business advertising dollars will be spent on the Internet (Clow and Baack, 2002). This section focuses on Internet communications. Mobile marketing and iTV marketing also have an increasingly important role in marketing communications. Their role is being discussed in the next section.

Essentially, the Internet can be used to send messages (e-mail), transfer data, monitor news and opinions, search and browse, and post, host, and present information (Keeler, 1995). This makes it a powerful marketing tool. Marketing can use the Internet for various purposes: research and planning, distribution, customer service, and marketing and corporate communications (Brassington and Pettitt, 2003). Marketing researchers and planners and the sales force can use the World Wide Web as a source of secondary information, i.e. to obtain marketing information about suppliers, clients, and prospects. Primary information through Internet surveys and the analysis of customer feedback and response can also be generated. The Internet can also be used as a direct sales and distribution channel (e-commerce). Through interactive websites orders can be taken, product offerings can be updated frequently, and customers can be stimulated to buy and pay online. Digital products such as videos, music and magazines can be distributed online, and tangible products can be ordered online and delivered at the address of the customer. Print and mailing costs and distribution costs (processing and handling) can thereby be reduced or eliminated. E-commerce also leads to *disintermediation*, i.e. the elimination of trade channel intermediaries, and can in that way also reduce costs. However, back office logistics and flexible IT systems have to be in place to enable real-time information flows and efficient fulfilment of orders. The Internet is also a powerful tool for developing and cultivating close links with customers and other target groups, for relationship and loyalty building, and for raising customer service levels. Customers can find up-to-date information, make inquiries and ask questions, and find the answers to their problems in the FAQ (Frequently Asked Questions) part of company websites. Sales persons can use the Internet as a sales support tool, i.e. to find information about clients and prospects, to communicate with clients, to disseminate information, stimulate purchases, take orders, and organize after-sales service.

Evidently, the Internet can also be used as a corporate and marketing communications tool. In corporate communications, the company website can be a PR medium to disseminate information about the company and its products to (potential) customers, investors, employees (internal communications, staff training), shareholders, governments, and various other stakeholders, to reinforce the corporate identity, to improve the company image, and to interact with these audiences. The company can be presented in a positive, entertaining, and amusing way. Basic information about the company (location, products, new jobs, etc.) can be communicated, questions about the company can be answered, and detailed old and current news releases can be made available in a cost-efficient way.

Finally, the Internet can also be used in marketing communications, through reaching customers directly, informing them, creating brand awareness, reinforcing brand image and brand attitudes, stimulating them to take action and try the product, and creating loyalty and building relationships with them (De Pelsmacker *et al.*, 2004) (Figure 8.1).

An important intermediary marketing communications objective is website traffic building. The Internet tool will be largely useless in obtaining its ultimate objectives if potential customers are not aware of the website, or do not know how to access it. Website traffic building will often imply substantial offline marketing communications support by means of mass media advertising and mentioning the website on packages, in-store communications tools and company stationery. Furthermore, website traffic can be stimulated by various forms of online communication such as advertising on other websites. Marketing communications on the Internet can take many forms, and often they mirror traditional communication tools. Besides brand sites, online advertising, online

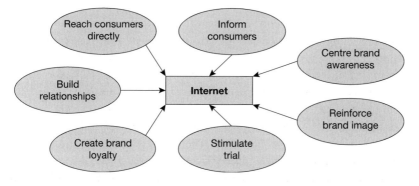

Figure 8.1 The Internet as a marketing communications tool

sales promotions, events and games, online direct marketing, and e-mail market-ing are used. These techniques and media are discussed in the next section.

It is important to understand that the Internet does not replace the traditional marketing and marketing communication tools, but supplements them. In fact, the Internet is a new medium that can (and should in many cases) be added to the marketing mix, but that is not capable of making any of the other marketing (communications) mix elements superfluous. However, because of its multimedia nature and its potential to engage in one-to-one interaction with potential customers, it can be a very powerful supplement to the traditional tools. Advertis-ing on the Internet can be made very creative and entertaining, corporate image building can be effectively enhanced, interaction via websites can be as tailor-made and personal as face-to-face contacts, direct marketing and sales can be stimulated as effectively as with traditional media, and customer care and customer services can be strongly supported. The evolution of digital technology enables the company to build and maintain powerful databases via the Internet that can be used for targeting specific and well-defined customer segments. In any case, the Internet should be fully integrated into the IMC mix, in terms of objectives, target groups and creative execution.

The Internet as a marketing communications tool has a number of strengths and limitations. They are summarized in Table 8.1. The main benefits of investing in e-marketing have been described as the five S's: sell, serve, save, speak, and sizzle (Smith and Chaffey, 2001; Smith and Taylor, 2002). Indeed, marketing through the Internet allows the company to directly communicate and interact with its customers one-to-one, sell them products and build relationships and loyalty, and convey lots of information at relatively low cost. The multimedia nature of the net allows the use of content, graphics, movement, audio and video, which can make Internet communications exciting and pleasurable. Furthermore, both the customer and the company can be quickly contacted at all times and at all places. Messages can be changed quickly and easily, and both customers and companies can save time. The Internet is a new advertising medium with a large and global audience potential, and it creates the opportunity to build sophisti-cated databases that allow precise customer segmentation and targeting.

However, the Internet also has its limitations. The potential reach of large customer segments is offset by the difficulty of identifying and finding them on the Internet. The actual reach and type of website visitors cannot always be tracked. As a result, the real impact of Internet communications is often uncer-tain. In fact, one of the challenges of e-marketing is to lead the target groups to the website, by means of offline communications or advertising on others' websites. This can be a costly operation. The nature of the medium requires that websites are professionally made and constantly updated. Again, this may be more expensive than anticipated. Integrating Internet communications in the IMC mix and in marketing strategy requires close cooperation between the marketing

Table 8.1 *Strengths and limitations of the Internet as a marketing communications tool*

Strengths	Limitations
■ Direct one-to-one contact	■ Poor targeting capabilities; reach and type of audience uncertain
■ Direct sales	■ What is the useful impact?
■ Communicate with loyal customers and reinforce relationship	■ Search difficulty: how can websites be found?
■ Interactivity	■ Need for offline and online communications support
■ Lots of information can be presented	■ Website development and maintenance costs
■ Low cost	■ Need for cooperation with IT department and call centre
■ Multimedia nature	■ Can create irritation
■ Shopping and other contacts can be made more pleasurable	■ Creative limitations?
■ Offers instant reach at any time and any place	■ Communication speed
■ Time saving	■ Buying behaviour inertia
■ Messages can be changed easily and quickly	
■ Possibility to advertise on others' websites	
■ Large audience potential	
■ Feed databases	

department, the IT department, and the customer contact centre. Too often, IT people build sites that cannot efficiently address the needs of marketers, or marketers launch campaigns that the website cannot technically cope with or the call centre and the back office cannot support. Some forms of Web communications, like banners and pop-ups are largely ineffective or irritate website visitors. Due to the immaturity of the medium, there are still a number of creative limitations. In most countries, the majority of the people do not have access to broadband technology. This limits the use of sophisticated multimedia applications, because they would result in irritatingly slow communication. Finally, the success of the Internet (and other new media) as a marketing tool depends upon the speed with which consumers are prepared to change their buying habits. If personal contacts and real shop visits are highly valued by the majority of the people, new marketing media will take off slowly.

115

e-communications techniques and media

An overview of the various e-communications techniques and media is given in Figure 8.2.

Brand websites are sites with specific brand-related information and/or services. They not only convey information, but also serve as a platform to interact with (potential) customers and to support other forms of Internet communications. Brand sites are also ideal vehicles to shape brand attitudes and brand images and to build relationships with loyal customers. They can make the brand experience richer and more exciting. Only famous and powerful brands can expect to spontaneously attract customers. Most brands will have to generate traffic to their brand sites by means of supplementary offline (in mass media, on packaging) and online (online advertising) communications and search engine optimization. They can be up and running continuously, but they can also be used to support temporary marketing campaigns or product launches. In the latter case, also *micro websites* are used. A micro site is a small website that exists for a specific purpose such as a product launch or a sales promotion campaign, and that can be reached via the main brand site, and other related sites, or that is promoted via offline advertising (De Pelsmacker *et al.*, 2004). The advantage is that specific campaigns can be detached from the main brand site. It makes the main site less heavy, and can lead specific target segments of the product launch or the promotion directly to simple and relevant messages. When the temporary action is over, the micro site can be easily removed without affecting the main site. For instance, Playstation has micro sites for every game, which are linked with the main site. Visa has developed micro sites on several portal sites, such as Yahoo and Geocities, with links to sites with themes such as skiing, music, shopping, restaurants, etc. The

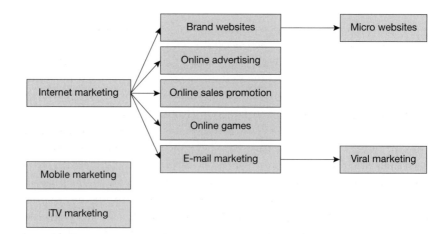

Figure 8.2 *e-communications techniques and media*

strategy was to lead potential Visa users to sites with relevant contexts and products for which Visa could be used.

Too often websites are designed by computer experts that do not take the marketing function and the target group of the site into account. Slow-loading front pages, numerous screens, too much verbal information, too many technical terms, sites that are hard to navigate, and tricky and clueless banners are all characteristics of poor web design (Clow and Baack, 2002). Studies indicate that people do not return to a website if it does not meet their expectations. A good website must be continually updated, easy to navigate, have relevant and in-depth information on its subject, offer interactivity, and quick loading and response times (Gaudin, 2002). In e-commerce applications, honesty, respect for privacy, reliability, and safety of payment are also highly regarded.

Online advertising is commercial messages in standard formats on rented spaces of other companies' websites. Its purpose is to build brand awareness and brand attitudes, and to generate traffic to the brand website. A multitude of techniques are used. *Banners* are graphic, sometimes animated, images used as advertisements. A button is a small rectangular or circular banner. A skyscraper is a thin and long banner along the right side of a web page. Online retailers such as Amazon use banners extensively in a technique that is called *affiliate networking*. Banners are placed on thousands of other sites, directing the visitor to the retailer's website. The banner-hosting website receives a commission every time someone clicks on the retailer's banner and buys something. *Pop-ups* are banners that appear in a separate window on top of a visited website. *Interstitials* are ads that appear temporarily when loading a new web page. They can cover the whole screen or only part of it. *Superstitials* are additional pop-ups that are opened when a new web page is opened. Pop-ups can be static or dynamic. In the latter case they contain animation, and are called *rich ads*. Pop-ups, interstitials, and superstitials are perceived as extremely irritating, but they also have the largest stopping power and performance, especially when they are in rich media (Briggs, 2001; Elkin, 2003). Banners are less irritating but hardly performant. *Advertorials* are banner or pop-up ads with an editorial approach, but a clearly identified sender. They are very similar to advertorials in traditional mass media. *Content sponsorship* is placing an online ad on a separate and very visible dedicated area of the website. *Homepage restyling* involves the adaptation of the look and feel of a web page into the colours and style of the advertiser. Finally, *anchor deals* are long-term cooperations between certain content sites and an advertiser. For instance, in exchange for co-branding on all Pepsi bottles, Pepsi advertised on the Yahoo website and Yahoo handled all the technical assistance for the Pepsi website (De Pelsmacker *et al.*, 2004). Another technique of online advertising is *keyword buying* on search engines. Search engines like Google enable web surfers to select web pages on the basis of search terms. Companies can buy the right for their ad to appear next to the search results for certain keywords. This technique

117

appears to be very performant and far less irritating than traditional banners (Elkin, 2003). Response rates for banner ads are extremely low and decreasing. They are estimated to be lower than half a per cent (i.e. less than 5 click-throughs for every 1,000 people that are exposed to the banner). This is due to banner clutter, bad media planning, and lack of creativity. Banners should be placed on related and relevant sites that target potentially interested visitors, and should creatively stimulate this visitor to click the ad.

Online sales promotion includes contests and sweepstakes, e-coupons, and e-samples. They can generate enthusiasm, build brand awareness, and reward loyal customers. They are often supported by offline communications (for instance in advertising and on packages), and can be used to enrich customer databases, if customers are asked to give their details before they can participate in the contest or receive coupons or samples. Due to the opt-in nature of most of these sales promotions (people have to indicate that they want to participate), the response can be very high, and they can be organized very cost-efficiently. Research indicates that more than 30 per cent of the web population uses online coupons, either by printing and using them or by redeeming them online (for instance to get a discount when buying online) (ACP, 2001).

Online games or advergames are rich media types of online brand-related enter-tainment. They use interactive game technology to link the brand to a pleasant and exciting web experience without explicitly advertising it. Games can drive traffic to the brand site and build brand image. Since they are not viewed as advertising and they are very involving, they can be very effective.

e-mail marketing is nothing more than using the Internet for direct marketing purposes. Just like in traditional direct marketing, e-mail marketing can be used inbound or outbound. However, direct marketing through the Internet allows customization, personalization, and niche targeting much more flexible, easier, quicker, and cheaper. Generally, e-mail marketing generates more response than traditional direct mail or online advertising. Click-through rates of e-mail marketing range between 2 and 10 per cent, but can be as high as 30 per cent if highly targeted and personalized (Waring and Martinez, 2002). However, the real threat for e-mail marketing is its overuse. Due to its low cost and its reputation for effectiveness, e-mailing has been used to bombard people with unsolicited and irrelevant junk mail ('spam'). Efficient e-mail campaigns should instead be based on carefully selected opt-in mailing lists, and should always offer the recipient the possibility to opt-out. Only then e-mailing is an excellent tool for *permission marketing*, a term used to indicate marketing actions that are based on the explicit permission of the target customer. A special form of e-mail marketing is *viral marketing* or *word-of-mouse marketing*. Messages are sent to a small and carefully selected target group of people who are potentially highly interested in the message. An advertising message is attached to the e-mail, and the recipient is asked to forward the e-mail and its attachment to friends. Viral marketing is based on the old principle that the most convincing form of advertising is the personal recommendation of a trusted friend (word-of-mouth). If successful, the message will be forwarded to thousands of people within days. The technique is also used on website banners and in online contests and games, and is similar to the member-gets-member programmes in traditional marketing. Viral campaigns work best if they are directed towards groups with strong common interests or lifestyles (affinity groups). Forwarding rates of more than 80 per cent have been reported, and studies indicate that more than 50 per cent of the recipients forward the message to 2 or more people (Clow and Baack, 2002). Their only disadvantage is that the marketer cannot control where the message is going or how it is distorted in the process.

Mobile marketing or *wireless advertising* uses mobile devices (mostly cell phones) to communicate with customers to promote products and services, using SMS (short messages) and MMS (multimedia messages). Usually the communication is opt-in, i.e. based on the permission of the recipient. Mobile marketing can be used to generate brand awareness, for contest and sweepstakes, to convey information, or to generate leads. Recipients are also able to call back for further information. Offline media, such as advertising and packaging, usually supports SMS campaigns. Research shows that mobile marketing can be extremely effective for generating brand awareness, building brand image, and generating interest and product trial (Enpocket Insight, 2003). The greatest danger is the extreme intrusiveness of wireless advertising. Therefore it should be used on a strict opt-in basis only. In the future, wireless location-aware advertising will also become possible, i.e. sending messages when a potential consumer is at the location where the product is offered (for instance a shop or a restaurant). Needless to say, besides being highly targeted and relevant, this form of advertising is potentially very intrusive.

Interactive television gives viewers the ability to interact with the programmes, view tailor-made content, and use a number of interactive services such as video-on-demand, home shopping, and home banking. *iTV marketing* offers marketers the opportunity to interact with the audience, for instance by offering interactive advertising. During the ad viewers can ask for more information, receive coupons or ask for samples, and even buy products. They can be asked to leave their details in order to enrich customer databases. Ads can be left on the electronic programme guide that is frequently visited by viewers. During an interactive commercial or linked to product placement viewers can be given the opportunity to visit a 'walled garden', i.e. a website that is exclusively linked to the programme. Companies can also sponsor programmes (programmercials), for instance a tour operator can sponsor a travel programme during which viewers can ask for more information about a trip or order one. The opportunities of iTV marketing are endless. Niche audiences can be targeted, one-to-one communications becomes possible, and new marketing channels can be opened.

119

However, the success of iTV marketing depends upon the evolution of technology, the penetration speed of digital television, and last but not least the willingness of television viewers to change their viewing patterns and to actively use the possibilities of interactive television.

The effectiveness of e-communications

Since e-communications are essentially a set of supplementary media to traditional marketing communications, it is imperative to fully integrate the new media into the IMC mix in order for them to be effective. The target groups, objectives, and messages of e-communications should be carefully integrated and consistent with the offline marketing communications instruments. Brand websites and online games or promotions should be supported by offline advertising campaigns or in-store communications. The online and offline build-up and maintenance of databases for direct marketing, personal selling, and relationship building should be consistent and integrated. Last but not least, e-communications campaigns should be coordinated efforts between the marketing and the IT department. Online applications should enable marketers to efficiently interact with their target groups, and marketers should only run campaigns that can be technically supported by the IT department.

The effectiveness of e-communication can be measured in a number of ways (Figure 8.3). The most basic type of measurement is to *ask for feedback* at the website, by leaving a contact e-mail address or inserting a feedback form. A more sophisticated technique is to carry out *online* or *offline visitor surveys*. They can be used to describe website user profiles (demographics and webographics – how they use the Internet), to analyse traffic and traffic generation, to measure product awareness, interest, knowledge and buying intention and current customer status, attitudes, satisfaction, and intentions. They can also be used to optimize the website in terms of information content, navigation characteristics, ease of interaction and transaction, service, and relationship building. Each time a web surfer clicks on a link, the server of the site will automatically record this in the server logfiles. *Logfile analysis* is very useful for tracking and analysing web surfing behaviour. The logfiles contain information on web page hits, time, frequency and number of visits, domains, browser types and platforms, web pages previously accessed, entry and exit pages, the number of unique visitors, and the names of the transmitted files (Sen, 1998; Bhat *et al.*, 2002; Weima, 2002; Chaffey *et al.*, 2003). Since it is impossible to identify specific users, website traffic is often analysed using *cookies*, pieces of software that are left on the user's PC and that enable websites to recognize the PC when it visits the site again. The effectiveness of online advertising and sales promotion can similarly be measured by means of the number of click-throughs that are generated, the number of interactions that are effectuated, or the redemption rate of e-coupons.

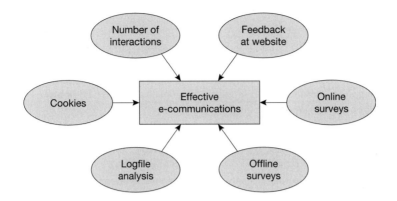

Figure 8.3 *Measuring e-communications' effectiveness*

SUMMARY AND CONCLUSION

Due to the impressive increase in the use of new media like the Internet and mobile phones, e-communications have become a vital part of the marketing communications mix in many companies. Online advertising and promotions, e-mail direct marketing, brand websites, and wireless advertising are valuable techniques to supplement and enrich the traditional marketing communications tools. e-communications can build awareness, improve brand attitudes, stimulate trial, and improve customer relationship management. The inherent interactivity of the new media gives them a unique place in the IMC mix. New technologies like interactive television hold the promise of revolutionizing marketing communications even more, because the receiver of the message will be able to customize it as he wishes. No doubt, in the future the role of new media in marketing will become more important, and new technologies and applications will emerge. For instance, some predict that new intermediaries will find a role for themselves, so-called 'infomediaries' that will collect information on customer preferences and purchases to build a holistic view of each individual consumer that can then be used by marketers and the customer himself (Tapp, 2002). As technology further develops, it is also predicted that the distinction between computers, televisions, and telephones will disappear. This is called media convergence. However, marketers must never forget that a new technology can only be successful when consumers are able and willing to understand, accept, adopt, and use it in their buying decisions.

121

QUESTIONS

- What are 'new media' and what are their most important characteristics?
- What is the role of e-communications in marketing?
- How can the Internet be used in marketing communications? What are its strengths and weaknesses?
- Discuss the various forms of Internet marketing communications and their strengths and weaknesses.
- How can the effectiveness of e-communications be enhanced and assessed?
- Develop an innovative integrated marketing communications campaign, using traditional media, the Internet, and wireless marketing.

Chapter 9

Relationship Marketing

LEARNING OBJECTIVES

After reading this chapter you will be able to:

- Assess the importance of relationship marketing
- Understand why customer relationship and customer contact management are important
- See how a relationship marketing database can be developed and maintained
- Understand how databases can be used to develop customer relationships by means of integrated marketing communications
- Assess the effectiveness of relationship marketing efforts, and appreciate the value of loyal customers

KEY TERMS

- Relationship marketing
- Customer relationship and contact management
- Database marketing
- Mass customization

Case study:
SOUTHWEST AIRLINES: HIGH-TOUCH–
LOW-TECH CUSTOMER RELATIONSHIPS

Southwest Airlines is an American airline that, contrary to most of its competitors, has been growing and profitable for 29 consecutive years. In 2001 it carried almost 65 million passengers on almost 1 million trips. The company has a fleet of 366 aircraft and employs more than 33,000 people. One of the reasons for its profitability is the strong loyalty of its customers. This loyalty cannot be explained by the airline's low prices alone. Southwest's customers are also very satisfied. In 2002 the company scored 74 out of 100 on the American Consumer Satisfaction Index, compared to an industry average of 66. This customer satisfaction, in turn, has been built up by means of a stringent focus on customer service and customer support. Southwest stays away from traditional airline CRM techniques, such as frequent flier perks and rewards for people who buy a lot of tickets. Every customer is equally important. Special groups of customers, such as businessmen seeking more legroom or reserved seats, are not particularly well accommodated. The company hires employees (both front desk and back office) primarily on the basis of their likeability and their ability to care and communicate.

Despite some new systems that help the planes depart on time (an important driver of customer satisfaction), the approach of Southwest is remarkably low-tech. It invested in CRM packages, such as a system to track and analyse customer data, but has decided that the benefits of this software did not outweigh the costs. The company also specifically rejects multi-channel tools that are heavily used by other airlines, e-mail response systems and interactive telephone menus, because they are too impersonal: they take the cost out of customer contacts, but also the quality. It is aware of the fact that, by following this strategy, it ignores one of the basic principles of CRM, i.e. that the customer should be able to reach the company how and when he wants. However, Southwest does not want to put a high-tech system in place if it does not adequately meet customer service requirements. This technologically conservative point of view may be in line with the strategy of high-touch personal service; it may also become a fundamental weakness in a competitive environment in which high-tech customer contacts are saving money that is reinvested in extra value for the customer (JetBlue, another low-cost airline, puts a satellite TV in each passenger's back seat).

Southwest has been a pioneer in paperless ticketing and online ticket selling, and it is well aware of the fact that in the future it will have to back up its high-touch approach with high-tech systems. Among other things, it is studying now how to gather more data about its customers, and how to use these data to offer better service. It also wants to develop CRM systems that enable sharing information between service counters and call centres. After all, Southwest do not pitch customer service just for the sake of the customer, but for the sake of the company. Good service is not meant to make customers smile, but to make customers come back.

Based on: Jeff Canon, Southwest Airlines: service for smiles and profits, www.crmguru.com, accessed 22 November, 2003.

Used with kind permission of Bob Thompson (CRMGuru.com).

OVERVIEW

Relationship marketing is a concept that stresses the importance of developing long-term win-win relationships with prospects and customers. It is a marketing (communications) approach that is aimed at establishing profitable relationships with loyal customers. In the first section the concept of relationship marketing and its importance for marketing communications is explained. Relationship marketing is based on structured customer relationship and customer contact management (CRM and CCM), the principles of which are discussed in the second section. CRM and CCM are based on well-designed and efficiently managed databases that contain customer characteristics, transaction and contact data, and that are used to plan communication campaigns more effectively. How to develop and use marketing databases is discussed in the third section. Databases can be managed to develop integrated marketing campaigns, such as frequency and permission marketing programmes. This is explained in the fourth section. Relationship marketing tries to develop impactful and profitable marketing programmes. The last section focuses on the effectiveness of relationship marketing efforts.

The importance of relationship marketing

The following definition of relationship marketing can be given:

> Relationship marketing is marketing seen as relationships, networks and interaction. It is aimed at establishing long-term win-win relationships with customers. In approaching a potential customer, relationship marketing has the ambition to climb the loyalty ladder: from prospect over first-time customer, to client, supporter, advocate and partner.
>
> (adapted from both Duncan, 2002 and Kotler, 2003;
> see also Figure 9.1)

Relationship marketing is the opposite of transaction marketing in which this ambition does not exist. Traditional transaction or acquisition marketing is short-term and sales-oriented and aims at the 'one shot deal' (Gummesson, 2000). It is aimed at converting prospects into customers, and nothing more. However,

125

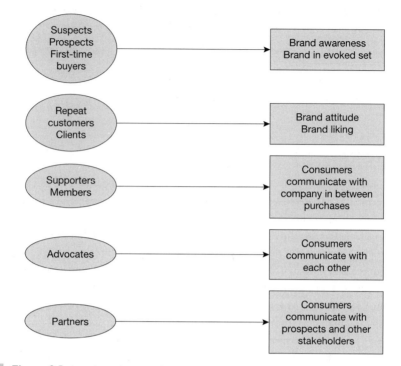

Figure 9.1 Levels and stages in customer relationships

marketing is not about selling, it is about making loyal customers. Relationship marketing is built upon the relationship between customer satisfaction, customer loyalty and profitability. It is five times cheaper to keep an existing customer than it is to acquire a new one, and some claim that substantial increases in profit can be realized by increasing customer retention by only a few per cent (Curry *et al.*, 1998). Therefore, companies should rather focus on retaining their existing customers, turning them into advocates and partners, than on the acquisition of new ones. True customer loyalty is more than just repeat purchases; it is having a share of wallet (the percentage of a customer's spending in a product category for your brand) as close to 100 per cent as possible. Relationship marketing is customer retention marketing. It is striving for zero defection. It implies caring for the existing customer first before trying to attract new customers. In that respect, also, successful branding is nothing more than building a special relationship between the customer and the brand: brand equity is brand value in 'stakeholder relationship' terms (Duncan, 2002).

Relationship marketing does not only apply to the relationship between the marketer and the customer, but also to all the company's stakeholders. That is when relationship marketing in fact becomes networking or marketing-oriented company management: managing the company with the customer in focus. A company does not buy and sell, individuals do. Therefore everyone in the company is a full-time or a part-time marketer, because even non-marketing staff have to act with the interest of the customer in mind. Therefore, it is, for instance, also important to keep good relationships with the distribution channel. Intermediaries are instrumental to understand the end-customers and to reach them effectively and efficiently.

Relationship marketing is based on a number of fundamental principles and factors. First of all, it is a long-term win-win collaboration with the customer. It is interactive in that it recognizes that all parties in the process are active, and it emphasizes relationship and service values rather than bureaucratic and legal values. Indeed, relationship marketers should try to do what is right from a long-term relationship perspective instead of hiding behind strictly legal considerations and technicalities (Gummeson, 2000). Relations imply collaboration, commitment, and dependency. Not all parties involved may be equally powerful, but those with less power still should have the feeling that they are better off than in another relation. Long-term relationships are the cornerstones of relationship marketing, and contacts between the marketer and the customer should be frequent, regular, intense, and as close as possible. This closeness can be physical, but also mental or emotional. Although a customer may only have contact with a marketer through a website or a direct mailing, he or she may feel close to the brand anyway. However, personal contact is critical for long-lasting high-quality relationships. High-tech will never make the need for high-touch obsolete. Physical proximity is as important as statistical or technical relationships. For instance, in a hotel the guests can fill out a customer satisfaction questionnaire, and the hotel management may or may not take the responses into account. Despite the physical proximity between the customer and the management, communication is strictly technical and statistical, and the quality of the contact is low-touch (Gummesson, 2000). However, hotels could also organize customer complaint or 'critical incident' conversations with their customers, making the contact more personal, interactive, and high-touch. Relationships quickly deteriorate when the romance and excitement has gone. Relationship marketing aims at customer delight and excitement, rather than just frequent routine contacts. High quality contacts imply regular value added, not only for the marketer, but also for the customer.

Finally, one of the most important components of high quality relationships with customers is trust. Brands and companies must be trusted before customers become loyal to them. The difference between repeat purchases and trust or loyalty is similar to the difference between brand or company image and reputation. Trust is built on satisfaction and satisfaction is based on the fact that goods, services, and employees perform as promised. When brands or companies promise more than they deliver, satisfaction and trust diminish. Relationship

127

marketing is therefore also customer expectations management: never promise the customer more than you can deliver. A second element in building trust is facilitating the interactivity with customers. Determining factors of trust are satisfaction, consistency, accessibility, responsiveness, commitment, affinity, and liking. Customers should be able to easily request information, make complaints, ask questions, and so on, whenever they feel like it, and the company should respond quickly and adequately to their queries. The most important objective in the relationship with dissatisfied customers is to restore trust. Marketing tools to build trust are, for instance, hot-lines, customer service departments, warranties, and guarantees (Duncan, 2002).

Relationship marketing implies a fundamentally different approach to integrated marketing communications than traditional transaction marketing (De Pelsmacker *et al.*, 2004). In a relationship marketing philosophy, integrated communications have to be aimed at retention and not just at acquisition. Selective interactive communications should be used instead of mass media monologues. Relevant information should be provided instead of repeated persuasive messages. Satisfaction and confidence in the company and its brands and meaningful relationships with customers should be built.

Customer contact and relationship management

In the old days, marketing and marketing communications were about following the AIDA scheme and building awareness and favourable attitudes, and influencing behaviour. Today, marketing and marketing communications is managing the customer contact experience. Customer Relationship Management (CRM) is defined as the process of managing detailed information about individual consumers and all customer 'touch points' with the objective of maximizing customer satisfaction, loyalty and profitability (Kotler, 2003). It is a combination of customer service and customer retention management. It is the company's promise that, in all customer contacts and no matter how customers interact with the company, the customer will always be recognized and receive the correct information and treatment (Duncan, 2002). This is sometimes described as Effective Consumer Response (ECR). CRM is sometimes referred to as Customer Contact Management (CCM): the coordination and management of all interactive communication between an organization and its (potential) customers. This communication may be in person, by telephone, mail, e-mail, or website (Pickton and Broderick, 2001).

Customer retention is one of the main objectives of CRM. The benefit of customer retention is higher profitability. The keys to customer retention are customer satisfaction and high switching barriers. Customers can be kept satisfied by delivering the goods and services they expect, or they can be prevented from running to the competitors by keeping switching barriers high (for instance making them lose loyal-customer discounts). Three retention-building approaches can be distinguished (Berry and Parasuraman, 1991):

- *Adding financial benefits.* For instance, frequency programmes reward repeat buyers and loyal customers. Club membership programmes (for instance the Harley Owners Group) create a closer bond between the customer and the company or the brand and result in extra financial benefits.
- *Adding social benefits.* Companies should have individual and professional contacts with their customers to turn them into real clients.
- *Adding structural ties.* It is not always realistic to count on customers being truly loyal. A firm tendency to repurchase is often the best a company can hope for. Therefore, adding structural ties (or increasing the barrier to switch) is often a useful component of CRM. The company can tie its customers to the organization by creating long-term contracts, by giving quantity discounts, and by engaging in long-term servicing relationships instead of selling products. For instance, a company could supply its customers with special equipment or access to the company's technology that enable them to order products and ask for assistance and service more easily.

The strategic implications of CRM are significant. CRM often implies a functional integration in the whole company. From the point of view of the customer, the company should appear seamless: all customer contacts should be consistently managed. Often, traditional marketing structures and departments have problems adapting to this new situation. Modern and efficiently organized CRM also creates the opportunity for reducing cost of sales and communications substantially. For instance, traditional sales persons cost approximately double the amount of money they earn (the rest is spent on offices, travel, accommodation). Only 6 per cent of their time is spent in front of a customer (Pickton and Broderick, 2001). Any alternative customer contact method is bound to be more cost-efficient. CRM can give rise to a multi-channel coverage strategy: lead generation, reselling, negotiation, administration, closing the deal, can all be covered through different CCM channels (mail, e-mail, website, telephone, personal call) on the basis of their cost-efficiency. CRM also offers the customer and the company the opportunity of more flexible two-way communications, thereby extending the choice over the means of contact and improving customer service. Last but not least, good CRM is technology-driven: digital communications, networked computer systems, web technology, call centres, and database technology should be integrated to make day-to-day CRM work. Relationship marketing should be based on a database that is well-designed and well-managed.

Database marketing: setting up a relationship marketing database

Database marketing is an interactive approach to customer contact management that is based on the accurate collection of (potential) customer, competitor and internal company information. Database marketing is the driving force behind relationship marketing and integrated marketing communications (Hartley and Starkey, 1996). A database is a collection of related information in computer files that is stored and organized to enable marketers to analyse, access, and produce information (O'Connor and Galvin, 1997; Fill, 2002). It can generate meaningful information and insights on customer behaviour and customer contact history: product buying behaviour; product use; customer complaints and remarks; new market trends; customer reactions to marketing communication efforts; and company reactions to customer behaviour (enquiries, buying, complaining). The database can also be used for computer-assisted sales support, direct response marketing, and customer information and service. It is a tool to help the sales staff, to assist in directly addressable and personalized communication ('chirurgical marketing', (Gummesson, 2000)), and to allow customers to contact the company quickly and easily and to get a quick and relevant response.

Database marketing involves two distinct types of activities. First of all, the database has to be developed and maintained. Second, it has to be used for relationship marketing and integrated marketing communications. The first component is covered in this section. The second is covered in the next section.

Setting up a database requires a number of decisions (Clow and Baack, 2002; Duncan, 2002):

- What data are needed? What and how much do we need to know about potential and actual customers? What specific pieces of information need to be included?
- How will the data be collected? Are we going to use internal and/or external information? How can the data be collected or purchased cost-efficiently?
- How will the data be stored and how efficiently can the stored data be processed and handled?
- How will the database be used? What analyses are needed? What kind of decisions will be based on these analyses? What kind of reports should we be able to make? What kind of activities should be supported by the database? How often will the database be used? Typical objectives and uses for a relationship management database are:
  - Providing useful information about (potential) customers.
  - Creating information about the factors determining purchase behaviour, and changes in buying behaviour and purchasing criteria used.

130

- Making an inventory of points of contacts with the customers.
- Yielding information about the role of each member of the decision-making unit.
- Targeting customers for direct marketing programmes.
- Helping the sales force to prepare prospecting, sales calls, and after-sales service.
- Assisting the customer relationship department in dealing with inquiries and complaints.

- Who will manage the database? What will be the involvement of the marketing and the IT department? How user-friendly should the database be? Who will have access to the database? Who will be able to add, change, and remove information?
- How accurate and secure does the database need to be? How frequently should it be updated and how confidential is the information?

In Figure 9.2, a possible architecture of a relationship-marketing database is given. It contains a number of types of data (De Pelsmacker and Van Kenhove, 2002; Duncan, 2002; Fill, 2002; Brassington and Pettitt, 2003). Besides customer identification data, the customer buying history is also stored. An important part of the database is the reaction of customers to marketing and marketing communication efforts: how did they react to direct mailing, reminders, advertising, sales promotions, etc. Also inbound and outbound contact data should be stored: when and how did they interact with the company or did the company interact with them, and for what purpose. This is collected in the contact section of the database. All this information is useful to analyse the database information and to build relevant and well-targeted IMC campaigns.

Database information can be collected in a number of ways. It can be based on external sources, such as externally purchased databases, government databases,

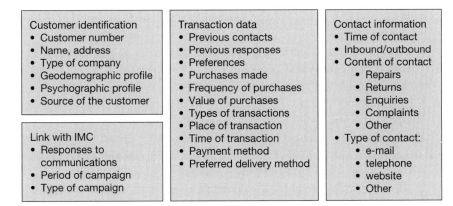

Figure 9.2 Types of information in a relationship-marketing database

or information collected by salespersons and middlemen such as distributors and other channel members. It can also be generated internally, through customer surveys, customer contacts (e-mail, telephone, website, etc.) and through the careful registration of transaction data. The latter is often the most important source of database information. Transaction data can and should be linked to marketing communication efforts such as advertising, direct mailing, website visiting behaviour, promotional offers, warranty cards, club membership, catalogues, toll-free numbers, and e-mails.

Companies should not just decide what type of information the database should contain, but also how it should be used and maintained. Database applications can be operational and analytical (O'Connor and Galvin, 1997; De Pelsmacker and Van Kenhove, 2002). In operational applications the database is used to help the company to collect data. Analytical applications allow the company to examine customer transactions and interactions, and to support the company to improve its relationships and transactions with its customers and stakeholders. These applications are often referred to as *data mining*. For instance, in analytical applications a model can be built to analyse how consumers reacted to marketing communication efforts, and predictions can be made on which customers should be approached and in what way to cross-sell to existing customers, to retain existing customers more effectively, and to improve relationships in general. Generally speaking, data mining tries to predict future behaviour based on previous buying behaviour or on developing profiles of customer groups that are promising. Questions such as the following can be answered:

- How much promotional money should be spent to attract new customers?
- What proportion of sales comes from which customers?
- Which customers might be receptive to cross-selling?
- Which customers should salespeople visit?
- What kind of efforts should be directed to high-, medium-, and low-value customers?
- What is the relationship between communication efforts and results with various customer groups?
- Which appeals and arguments are most effective with different target groups?

Obviously, the most important benefit from database development, maintenance, and use is the support it can give to integrated marketing communication efforts.

Database management, relationship marketing, and integrated marketing communications

From an IMC perspective customers have relationships with both products and companies. Databases are the tools that enable companies to do integrated marketing communications, and allow them to support the 'customer first' philosophy (Duncan, 2002). It allows companies to register each contact with each individual (potential) customer at each point in time via each communication channel. It allows analysis of this data stream in order to increase sales after the first contact was made, to keep regular contact, and to develop a range of activities (from direct mails to sales calls) to encourage further buying and become or stay loyal to the company. Therefore, database management is at the core of customer relationship management and IMC programmes. Consequently, database management is not just about giving support to direct marketing campaigns. Direct marketing is only one of the communication instruments of relationship marketing. Also telemarketing, call centres, e-mails, and websites can be used. Furthermore, database information can give support to advertising and sales promotion managers by giving them insight into customer characteristics, attitudes, preferences, and buying behaviour (Clow and Baack, 2002).

An important component of database-driven communication is *mass customization*. This means personalizing the interaction between a company and a (potential) customer on a large scale. In its simplest form it is using the name of the customer in communication (telephone calls, letters, and so on). On a second level, the communication refers to previous transactions (complaints, enquiries, orders, etc.). The most sophisticated variant is when a solution is offered to the specific problem of the customer. For instance, at the Ritz-Carlton hotels each employee is trained to keep track of the guests' likes, dislikes, and habits. The data goes into a database, and is combined with the buying history of the customer, e.g. when and where did he stay in one of the hotels, which discounts did he benefit from, what other things did he buy. Each of the 240,000 repeat customers is treated individually by the staff of the hotel, using the information stored in the database. Database technology makes mass customization possible, personal contact also makes it customer-friendly (Gummesson, 2000).

Databases can be used for monitoring and steering marketing communication campaigns in a number of ways. The links between the stages in an IMC campaign and database management are summarized in Figure 9.3 (Duncan, 2002).

Databases can also be used in different stages of the relationship between a customer and a company or a brand (Duncan, 2002; Brassington and Pettitt, 2003). In the *acquisition stage* the database can be mined to compose demographic, psychographic or behavioural segments that may be interesting target groups for a new offer. In the *customer growth stage* the database should be used to encourage the customers to buy more of the same product category (selling up) or products

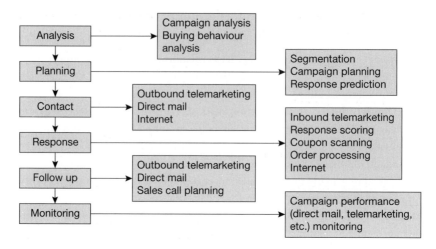

Figure 9.3 *Stages in an IMC campaign and database management*

from a different category (selling across). Certain customer segments can be approached by means of cross-selling offers, special promotions or telemarketing. In the *retention stage* it is important to not only renew the contact with the customer on a regular basis, but also to listen to customers and to respond to their enquiries and complaints and do something about it. The database can be screened to find out about particular customers that should get immediate and intensive attention, and be contacted in the way they prefer. Finally, in the *reacquisition stage* companies should try to use the database to minimise churn (customer defection). The first step is to discover as quickly as possible when they have defected. Next, they can be contacted to find out how they can be convinced to become a customer again.

In the acquisition stage, but also in the other stages, *permission marketing* is becoming increasingly popular. In a permission marketing programme the company sends messages and offers only to customers that have given the company the explicit permission to do so. In that way, the company does not intrude on consumers who do not want to receive e-mails, telemarketing calls, or catalogues. It forces the company to engage in relevant and value-adding interaction with their customers. Permission marketing communications often generate higher responses, they are less expensive than traditional forms of communication, and they result in stronger relationships with customers. Permission marketing does not only allow the company to acquire customers, but also to make them more frequent and loyal buyers. A number of steps have to be followed in developing a permission-marketing programme (Godin, 1999). First of all, the permission has to be obtained. This is often done by offering the customer an incentive (cash, a prize, information) in return for his or her cooperation. Consequently, the customer gradually has to be offered more and more information about the company and its products. The third stage is to reinforce or change the incentive to further appeal to customers and to continue the relationship. For instance, a range of benefits may be offered to the customer who buys more, or more frequently. Customers can also be invited to have an impact on the incentive they receive (by giving them the chance to make a choice themselves). Concurrently, the company can increase the level of permission. The customer can be asked for more information in return for more valuable incentives. Demographic, lifestyle, and buying behaviour information can then be integrated into the database to allow more fine-tuned segmentation and communication. Finally, the permission can be leveraged to benefit the company and the customer. In this stage the customer becomes brand- or company-loyal and is willing to provide extra information. The company can enhance this relationship by making the customer feel special and 'part of the club' (for instance by regularly offering him or her special benefits). When the company introduces and supports *membership programmes*, customers can become or stay part of a specially created club. A club is normally based on loyal buying behaviour and frequent contacts with the company. Rewards can be discounts, special offers, and access to special products and services. The purpose of membership programmes is to build long-term relationships with the members of the club. For instance, airline loyalty programmes offer benefits (free miles, upgrading) based on loyalty. The more intense the relationship between the airline and the customer becomes, the more benefits the member of the loyalty club gets. After some time he is upgraded to gold or platinum member, and gets even more extra miles and upgrades (Gummesson, 2000).

In many cases it is not possible to make the majority of the customers loyal, because they are not (or cannot be made) involved enough with the product category, or the differences between brands or companies are not very obvious. In such cases repeat purchase is the best the company can hope for, and the company should develop *frequency programmes*. This is an incentive plan to stimulate customers to make repeat purchases (Clow and Baack, 2002). For instance, most airlines and hotel chains have frequency programmes. Although they have the potential of becoming relationship-building tools, for many people airline tickets and hotel rooms are low involvement services that are not very much differentiated from the competition. In these circumstances, people often buy the product because of the incentive, not because of the intrinsic quality of the product itself or because of their quality relation with the company. The goal of a frequency programme is to maximize a customer's motivation not to switch to a competitive offer in the most cost-efficient and profitable way. The offer to the customer should be simple and easy to understand, the marketing database should be extensively used to maximize the impact of the programme, feedback to the offer should be stored in the database, and at all times the profitability of the programme should be monitored.

135

Permission marketing, frequency and loyalty programmes can be developed using both traditional and electronic media. Often, each tool will have a role to play in the integrated relationship marketing communications effort. However, the specific characteristics of the Internet can be used to build web-based relationship programmes. For instance, Dell provides a Premier Pages service for its corporate clients. Each Premier Page is a separate website that is dedicated to a particular customer, and only accessible by that particular company. It holds a record of all customer information and all previous transactions between Dell and that customer. This information is used by Dell to communicate and make tailor-made offers to each individual company (Jobber and Fahy, 2003). *Communities* are groups of people with common interests that interact and share experiences. They can be ideal vehicles to build relationship with a company and its products. In a way, they can become the electronic version of membership clubs. Companies can set up such a community themselves, or they can try to associate with an existing community. Examples of communities are parentsoup. com (for parents) and rankit.com (a community for young people initiated by Visa).

The effectiveness of relationship marketing

Short-term profits are an outcome of long-term investment in relationships and consequently one should prioritize the long term (Gummesson, 2000). It costs less to sell to current customers, relationships amortize acquisition costs, and a small decrease in customer defection leads to a large increase in sales and profits. Defected customers can cause other customers to leave, while loyal customers are more profitable and require less handholding. Disappointed customers cause negative word of mouth, while loyal customers are company and brand advocates (Duncan, 2002). Relationships also increase the value of the customer. All of these are reasons to believe that relationship marketing is more effective than transaction marketing. The concept of *lifetime customer value* is used to describe the estimation of how much a customer contributes to the company's profit over the years he or she buys from the company. This is sometimes called the 'return on relationship' (Gummesson, 2000). The ultimate purpose of relationship marketing should be to maximize this lifetime value for every customer (Jenkinson, 1995; Reichheld, 1996; Curry *et al.*, 1998).

In a more hands-on fashion, the effectiveness of database marketing efforts is often measured by means of the *Recency-Frequency-Monetary Value* (RFM) model. In the RFM approach three indicators are monitored for each customer: the time elapsed since the last purchase, the frequency with which a customer places an order, and the average amount of money a customer spends per purchase. For each variable a number of categories can be defined, and the target group of, for instance, mail shots or telemarketing campaigns can be defined based on

136

previous experiences with the response rates of different categories. The response information (enquiries, purchase, amount, etc.) can be fed into the database to make future IMC campaigns even more effective (see for instance Rapp and Collins, 1990).

Finally, a word of caution is in place regarding the profitability of relationship marketing. The logic behind the concept is that brand performances that exceed expectations lead to satisfied customers, who will in turn become loyal, buy more, and become highly profitable. However, large and loyal customers are not always the most profitable ones. It takes a lot of effort to make customers satisfied and loyal, and once they are, it takes investments to keep them loyal. Often, a so-called 'service paradox' is found: more satisfied and loyal consumers are less profitable (Gummesson, 2000). Therefore, individual customer profitability should always be monitored.

To manage the effectiveness of relationship marketing, the following things should be kept in mind (Gummesson, 2000):

- Customer satisfaction is not a guarantee for customer loyalty: delight the customer.
- High customer perceived quality and satisfaction is not enough: customers have to be continuously encouraged to stay.
- Dissatisfied customers do not necessarily run away; satisfied customers do not necessarily stay: active retention programmes are a necessity.
- Satisfaction indicators should be interpreted with caution. Sometimes repeat buyers are just 'happy slaves': they are not currently aware of alternatives.
- Satisfied customers are not necessarily profitable.

Case study:
HOW TO TURN $25 INTO $4,000 WITH CLEVER RELATIONSHIP MARKETING

Get Organized Now! is a one-person consultancy in the US that markets organizing services to individuals and businesses. Most small companies place advertisements in local newspapers to promote their business, but this approach is often not very effective. Maria, the owner of the company, decided that she wanted to build a prospect list of people with a high interest in getting organized. She contacted another local business that had conference rooms that could be rented by the hour. Instead of paying for a room, Maria made the following offer. She would offer a free workshop (worth $35 per person) provided she could use the room for free, and the conference room owner would include an invitation to the workshop in his next invoice mailing. The conference room owner perceived this as a win-win situation: he was able to offer his clients a $35 workshop for free and his clients would get valuable organizing information. Maria and her services would get an introduction to a new group of potential customers.

The mailing and subsequent calls resulted in seventeen people attending the workshop. Of course, the main purpose of the workshop was to obtain the contact information of all the attendants. Therefore, Maria composed a documentation pack, worth $25. People could sign up for this free documentation, but had to leave their full contact data. At the cost of $25 she now had 17 prospects that already knew and liked her services, and with whom she had already built trust. Next, she called all of them, offering them more free organizing tips, and leaving them information about her services and fees. Three companies made an appointment, one of which became a customer and ordered a $585 project. Another new client was a referral from an attendee at the workshop. This client ordered three consultancy services for a total of $1,500. Within eight months of the initial free workshop, the company received over $4,000 in organizing project fees. Over the next couple of years, repeat sales and additional referrals increased that amount substantially.

The 'Get Organized Now!' approach worked because a number of principles of good relationship marketing were used: create interest by means of an irresistible offer; attract prospects by means of a win-win proposition; offer an incentive to get contact information; follow up on prospects by getting appointments and making new customers; keep customers satisfied and loyal, they will be advocates for your business.

Based on: Joe Gracia: How you can turn $25 into $4,000, Give to Get marketing, www. givetogetmarketing.com, accessed 22 November, 2003.

Used with kind permission of Give to Get Marketing.

SUMMARY AND CONCLUSION

Satisfied customers become loyal, and loyal customers are more profitable. Relationship marketing tries to optimize individualized communications and interactions with customers and prospects to develop a long-term profitable relationship with them. Relationship marketing uses a multitude of channels: direct mailings, e-mails, telemarketing, and the Internet are the most commonly used to reach, convince and communicate with customers more effectively, to support sales staff efforts, and to enhance customer service. But most of all, relationship marketing is technology-driven: database and data mining technology combined with call centre and web technology, enable the marketing (communications) manager to efficiently develop customer contacts. A relationship marketing database contains customer characteristics, transaction and contact data, and allows analyses that enable the marketer to more efficiently reach specific target groups with the right offer, and turn them from first-time buyers into loyal customers and advocates. Permission marketing and frequency programmes are specific marketing communications approaches to relationship marketing. The effectiveness of relationship marketing depends on the extent to which customers can be kept satisfied and loyal in a profitable manner.

QUESTIONS

- Why is relationship marketing important and how does it relate to company profitability?
- What are the objectives of customer relationship and customer contact management and how does it relate to integrated marketing communications?
- What are the components of a relationship-marketing database and how can it be developed?
- How can a database be used to develop marketing communication campaigns?
- What is permission marketing and how can it be developed?
- How can frequency programmes be developed?
- How can the effectiveness of relationship marketing be assessed?

Chapter 10

Summary and Conclusion

LEARNING OBJECTIVES

After reading this chapter you will be able to:

- Develop a greater understanding of IMC: how it is defined, explained, practised, and defended
- Gain insight into how different promotional mix elements can be *integrated* at least at one level (see Figure 1.1, Chapter 1)
- Gain insight into how marketers, and servicing agencies, can move upwards through an IMC developmental process
- Develop an overview of the role of creativity in all media neutral communication solutions

KEY TERMS

- Integrated marketing communications (IMC)
- IMC – defined, explained, practised, defended
- Promotional mix
- Creativity
- Media neutral communication

INTRODUCTION

As with all other chapters, we commence with a case study. Unlike many other cases, Audi, and their agencies, have moved beyond simple juxtaposition of promotional mix elements. Can you identify how they have done this?

Case study: AUDI UK

Integrated creative thinking at Audi has enabled the brand to buck tough trading conditions and boost both its profile and sales through a new, more inclusive brand strategy.

Audi is one of Germany's oldest car manufacturers. Its product philosophy is to produce cars which are attractive, sophisticated, and technically perfect. Its approach is underpinned by an innate sense of creativity, commitment, and enthusiasm. And its declared aim is to lead through innovation, to set new standards to substantiate the statement 'Vorsprung durch Technik' — a motto first seen above the main gate of Audi's German factory long before it became an advertising line.

Product design has long been at the heart of Audi's business, and this has had a major impact on internal culture and its brand positioning. By the late 1990s, however, it was apparent that simply saying Audi products have great design was not enough. While a core audience understood where the brand sat in the market the majority were unable to articulate what it stood for.

Until then, Audi's brand strategy had been to celebrate what it wasn't. It wasn't flash; it wasn't gauche; it wasn't BMW. Following a spate of mergers between car companies, the introduction of 'platform production strategies', and the sheer speed with which one competing car company can now emulate product features introduced by another, brand rather than product differentiation had become the business' key driver. The Audi brand needed to be more obviously and positively defined as something tangible.

In 2000, design moved centre-stage within Audi UK branding with the creation of a 'communications platform' around the theme of great design — not just in the automotive arena. This integrated communications strategy — ranging from advertising and direct marketing to strikingly-designed household items made from car components — has re-positioned and re-vitalized the Audi brand, challenging the perceptions of consumers and Audi employees throughout the UK. It also won Audi four Silver awards at D&AD's 2003 awards and inclusion within the 2003 annual in a variety of categories, including Integrated Creativity for a striking piece of direct mail constructed from an Audi car part.

141

An ability to cater for the expected and unexpected

There are two key strands to Audi UK's repositioning, one planned the other not. The planned strand is the more traditional – a brand communications comprising new advertising, point of sale, and direct marketing materials developed by Audi UK's advertising agency, Bartle Bogle Hegarty.

The unplanned strand is unconventional. The Audi Uncovered Design Initiative is an experimental art and design collection bringing to life the new brand positioning. It was developed by brand experience consultancy Jam who approached Audi on spec having seen the first wave of BBH's repositioning work.

Design: a single, uniting creative theme

Conventionally, Audi, like other car brands, mixed occasional 'brand theme' campaigns with an array of product-specific communications each with a different idea, endline, and look. A new communication model was introduced which put the brand at the centre of every piece of communication which would now share a consistent look, message and theme. Future cars would be launched not as Audi sub-brands but new examples of Audi's overall brand message.

Design already played a major role – in terms of product design – within the Audi business. The time seemed right to move the concept of design centre-stage in branding terms to become the single, uniting theme for every piece of Audi UK brand communi-cation. 'Audi's commitment to fostering design and creativity has contributed to a culture which works in favour of the brand and branding requirements,' says BBH director of planning, Guy Murphy.

BBH identified an association with the ultimate fusion of form and function as perfectly in tune with the aspirations of prospective and existing Audi customers. This was also in tune with growing moves within Audi to associate more closely with design at other levels. In 1997 the company launched the Audi Foundation (now called the Audi Design Foundation) to provide bursaries to help young British designers bring their product ideas across all product categories – not just design – to life.

Catering for the unexpected

The new strategy launched in mid-2000 with a series of ads. The first, 'Phonebox', was a TV commercial featuring not a car but a futuristic phone box designed by Audi's chief car designer, Romulus Rost. The aim was to demonstrate Audi's understanding of form and function to create great design. This was supported by a mixed media campaign with press and posters juxtaposing great pieces of design with Audi products, and point of sale materials featuring great designs, such as a silver coffee pot, with no cars at all. Even direct mail shared the theme.

What happened next, however, was completely unplanned.

Design innovators at Jam saw 'Phonebox' on TV and contacted Audi on spec. Although unused to responding to cold calls, former Audi UK marketing director Rawdon Glover agreed to a presentation by Jam – and ended up investing a small amount of money to enable Jam to develop concept designs. 'The idea was to give them a chance to show what they could do. It was a brave move – completely unconventional', says Audi UK events marketing manager Nick Broomhall. 'But it was also relatively low risk as it was low key, although once we saw Jam's ideas we quickly saw the potential'.

Jam produced a series of household items made from car components, including a wine holder made from a cylinder block; a magazine rack fashioned from a spring; even a toilet roll holder that was once a wing mirror. 'The question was: just how can you bring to life the value of the design positioning?' Jam chief executive Jamie Anley explains:

> The initial aim of our work was to create something that could bring alive the design positioning of the Audi brand to people in showrooms throughout the UK. What happened shows how things can take on a momentum of their own, and how a company can capitalise on that if it thinks and acts fast enough.

Media neutral creative solutions

Audi UK's long-standing relationship with BBH ensures both integrated and 'media neutral' creative solutions. BBH prides itself on working across all channels and the team working on the Audi account – and BBH's creatives – have a breadth of experience. As a result, the response to all briefs is to create one big idea which can be brought to life by many different media channels.

To achieve this, BBH's account team works closely with a dedicated, skilled set of people within the agency responsible for data targeting, data purchase, and campaign analysis. This specialist data planning team is involved in every campaign. Direct marketing for Audi is also created and produced within BBH by a dedicated DM production team. BBH also manages stand-alone direct mail activity for existing customers, third-party promotions, and event invitations.

When Audi put BBH and Jam together it was with the expectation that the two would collaborate closely and the concept design initiative filter across into a range of other brand communications.

Integrated creativity – and implementation

With Jam's work well under way, BBH's next advertising and direct marketing materials comprised simple yet striking images of car components lit and photographed as if they were jewellery featured in a glossy brochure. Each item was set against a black

143

background and accompanied by the component's product code. 'Great design but just a random part you'll never see', was the unspoken line.

Jam's range of twelve products was officially launched mid-summer 2002. It went on display at Audi's permanent showroom, The Forum, in London's Piccadilly, and the plan was for a collection to be on show at selected Audi Centres in coming months. Meanwhile, BBH created a further series of ads – depicting Jam's items. Ensuing PR interest spanned a diverse range of media from *Design Week* and *Blueprint* to *Top Gear* and the *Sunday Times*.

Jam then worked with BBH to produce a unique piece of direct mail for loyal Audi customers. Audi uses direct mail to target different car owners, notably those about to buy a new car; those mid-way through their ownership cycle – typically assumed to be 18 months after purchase; and those about to replace their existing model. Jam created an iconic talisman – a reproduction of a headlight lens from an A4 and roll-over bar from a TT Roadster – for use as a paperweight or magnifying glass. The first 3,000 were mailed to customers in early summer 2003.

'The new positioning, and Jam's work especially, has given us credibility and allowed us access to places we'd not otherwise have been allowed to go – such as a founding sponsor of Gateshead's new gallery, the Baltic Contemporary Arts Centre', Broomhall says. 'Anyone can claim "We are the design brand", but you've got to act it to be credible. All of this activity provided us with a powerful brand communications platform'.

Through a closely integrated communications strategy ranging from advertising and direct marketing to household products made from Audi car components – Audi was able to communicate a clear positioning.

The first phase of Audi's design strategy began in 2000. Analysis of UK sales in 2002 show a year-on-year increase of 21.3 per cent in unit sales. Meanwhile, Audi's share of the total UK market went up, from 2.2 per cent to 2.65 per cent.

While it's difficult to attribute this solely to the new brand communications strategy, it has certainly contributed to this positive performance in extremely tough trading conditions in the UK automotive market.

Meanwhile Audi's unbranded recognition was, on average, 24 per cent higher than other car brands' following the strategy's launch, and branded recognition 35 per cent higher. Pre-launch, no one ever spontaneously talked about Audi and design; post-launch it was the most cited aspect of communication (Source: Hall & Partners).

Traffic to Audi's website during the 5 months after the launch of the new strategy rose by 75 per cent compared with the 5 months preceding it (Source: Goodtech).

Source: Taken from a 2003 D&AD (British Art, Design, and Direction) *Creativity Works Case Study*, written by Meg Carter. We acknowledge with gratitude their kind permission to cite this material here.

INTRODUCTION ... *continued*

The question with which we opened the chapter is fairly straightforward. The answer in IMC terms takes some untangling. Note:

1 Audi UK deliberately set out to build an integrated communications strategy.
2 They sought to use all pertinent promotional mix elements, leading to an overall brand message.
3 Creativity was evident in all phases of development. Serendipity (i.e. Jam) was a hallmark following initial repositioning.
4 The campaign(s) relied for their integrity on underlying product design, backed by appropriate pricing, and quality distribution.
5 The company, BBH, and Jam worked closely together to develop media-neutral solutions.
6 The campaign was underpinned by a clear understanding of market dynamics, including different buyer types.
7 The positioning adjustment worked, and led to behavioural outcomes, as well as the usual attitudinal criteria.

While there is insufficient data in the case study to warrant that Audi had moved through all stages of Figure 1.1, there is evidence that there is strategic movement in all phases of the Figure.

Let us now assess where we are in the primer journey of IMC. By now you should have developed greater understanding, insight, and an overview of what IMC is and how the various promotional mix elements can be integrated.

Understanding

IMC is not, and may never be, a uni-dimensional concept. Instead, it is multi-dimensional, depending in all cases on where the market happens to be at a specific point in time. Using a life-cycle analogy, IMC is already in the theoretical mature stage in its birth nation, i.e. the USA. In terms of practice, however, it is still in the growth stage. Elsewhere, the UK for example – where this book is published – it is also theoretically mature, but in practical terms still in its infancy. In the mind of each marketer, agency practitioner, student, and academic commentator, IMC may occupy a slightly different space. That space is conceptualized in Figure 10.1.

Marketing communicators

For the marketing communicator, at any point in time, their market will be surrounded by the usual macro and micro environmental forces. The marketing

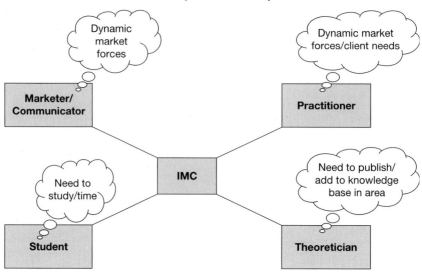

IMC Conceptual/Practical Space

Figure 10.1 IMC conceptual space

group will be accountable – either to the strategic business unit or corporate management in terms of performance, and in relation to budget requirements. Thus, though progression through various levels of IMC may be seen as advantageous and beneficial, the argument that proves its efficacy and bottom-, middle-, and top-line contribution may be difficult to marshall, and even more difficult to generate resource to truly implement IMC. Thus, it may be necessary to settle for IMC at a lesser level (e.g. 1, 2, 3) *for the time being*. As recounted in *Marketing Mind Prints* (Kitchen, 2004), there is clear evidence that despite all the training and dissemination of the marketing concept – for over four decades now – most UK firms are simply poor in terms of marketing. So, if marketing itself is not widely disseminated or fully applied, then for its lesser offspring – IMC – it is unlikely that this will be fully understood either.

Practitioners

By 'practitioners', we refer to all those agency personnel in advertising, sales promotion, direct marketing, marketing PR, and the like, who service the needs of brand and corporate marketing in pursuit of marketing and corporate communication objectives. In many cases (e.g. Audi UK), a very close working relationship builds between client and agency. Generally, the closer this relationship the greater the trust, and the greater the likelihood that clients will entrust agencies to move ahead with potentially all stages of an IMC campaign – from market evaluation and measurement of customers and prospects, to design of messages, purchase and dissemination through media to appropriate contact points and measurement of behavioural and attitudinal outcomes. That is the ideal. In many cases, however, clients may not entrust all their marketing communications to one agency. Do we believe that agencies can implement IMC campaigns (at all stages and levels)? The answer is 'yes'. As agencies, however, they can only do what clients ask them. They are agents, not principals. In a number of studies carried out between 1997 and 2003, Kitchen, Schultz, and others (see Kitchen and Schultz, 2003; Kitchen and Li, 2004; Kitchen et al., 2004) discovered that agency personnel understood what IMC is, what benefits it can provide to clients, and are capable of creative design, message delivery, and evaluation. But, in many cases, clients may not draw upon all available integrated expertise. The agencies too are exposed to market forces, many of which require them to *actually be* integrated and offer through-the-line media-neutral services.

Theoreticians

There are numerous expositions, definitions, and even opposition to, IMC, and numerous explanations of its developmental process, and how and in what ways it might be applied. Certainly we feel that IMC is just beginning to be understood, though it is definitely the preferred and recommended norm in terms of client and agency practice and in the marketing and marketing communications literature.

Students

Students are always constrained by time, hence we have provided in the Appendix (see p. 151) a lengthy section on study techniques, to use more advantageously the time you have. There is a need to study IMC, as it appears to be one of the most significant developments in marketing at the end of the twentieth century and furthermore, interest in IMC shows no sign of abatement in the twenty-first. We would urge and encourage you to study IMC, monitor its development, and see how best it can be applied in the organizations you work for. We also encourage active research in this area, in order to push forward the boundaries of knowledge.

Insight

Insight into the domain of IMC is now a matter of extensive and intensive study as there is so much information available about it. Many of the models expounding and explaining IMC in terms of development, application, explanation, and evaluation require further testing in the field of actual application. We applaud the great work of D&AD, the IPA, CIM, and all of the research centres and individuals who are generating insight into this topic, without which of course this book would not exist. Surprisingly, insight into marketing comes from many diverse disciplines, and the greatest insights are related to actual exchange processes in real markets. Let me share a quotation from Virginia Woolf (1984):

> Examine for a moment an ordinary mind on an ordinary day. The mind receives a myriad of impressions – trivial, fantastic, evanescent, or engraved with the sharpness of steel. From all sides they come, an incessant shower of innumerable atoms; and as they fall, as they shape themselves into the life of Monday or Tuesday, the accent falls differently from the old; the moment of importance came not here but there.

We are in the process of developing insight into a new and emergent paradigm – IMC. Driven by market forces, it has significantly altered the ways companies, agencies, and media vehicles develop, implement, and evaluate communications. It represents a needed critique of the marketing concept, by indicating that 'inside-out' communications is no more than the old sales orientation dressed in new clothes. A simple move from stage 1 to stage 2 of the IMC model (see Figure 1.1) represents a startling change in ways of thinking about and acting upon market data – or information about primary sources of growth and profit i.e. customers. IMC has ramifications well beyond its original foundations in the promotional mix. For, its real foundations lie in customers, consumers, and prospects. That is maybe why we need to examine our ordinary minds on ordinary days. Are we really examining ways to improve our marketing and communication? Or, are we gazing into the reflexive mirror of organizational-driven edicts, without stopping to find out where the accent in communications lies?

OVERVIEW

Let me conclude with another quotation from a marketing thinker who had his mind fixed on the capacity of marketing to survive and drew upon a biological analogy:

> The best analogy for the capacity of a system to survive is the health of a biological organism . . . it is rational to exercise proper care to keep the body or the system healthy. The prime strategy is . . . a strategy of avoidance. The individual tried to avoid infection or other conditions that might cause illness. Through occasional medical examination he hopes for early

detection of what might otherwise become an incurable and fatal disease. The executive watches for maladjustment in the system and attempts to provide proper remedies.

(Alderson, 1964)

Certainly the time and circumstances for the emergence of IMC were opportune. In the 1990s marketing found itself exposed to microscopic attention in terms of what it does and how it is done, and required proofs of outcomes in hard financial terms. The ideal of marketing, that it is somehow related to the needs and wants of target customers – and of firms developing skills to satisfy these needs more effectively and efficiently than the competition – is well documented. But, IMC seems to provide a lens or focus in which first communication can be sharpened and honed, and then extend to greater development in the ways marketing is structured and managed within companies. IMC seems to be a proper remedy to the maladjustments in the marketing system, but not, we hasten to add, at stage 1 of its development.

CONCLUSION

IMC has proven to be of significant value in many dimensionalities. It is not a static concept. As a squalling infant is capable of many societal contributions as an adult, so IMC itself seems to have progressed rapidly and is now 'under fire'. We suspect the 'fires' of application, analysis, and criticism, will serve to strengthen the theoretical and practical foundations of the subject. We certainly hope that this has been the case for readers of this short text.

QUESTIONS

Just three questions. All relate to one anonymous quotation:

The sermon had ended
The priest had descended
Delighted were they . . .
But, they preferred the old way.

(Anon)

149

1 How might this apply to IMC?
2 How might it apply to the stages theory of IMC?
3 Please extend the application to a critique of the communications of a company of your choice. Where do they fit in the IMC model? Or, in the context of the above quotation?

ACKNOWLEDGEMENT

We gratefully acknowledge D&AD and Meg Carter for allowing us to include the Audi UK case in this chapter.

Study Guide and Techniques

If you are a marketing communications student you are likely to be interested in how to study effectively and how to communicate well. In this Primer, topics have been refined to key issues to help you gain a rapid grasp of integrated marketing communications and each subject area. The short sections below are written to expand this grasp by suggesting *how to make studying more effective*. It also contains *guidance to help gain good grades* by using presentation tips.

CONTENTS

1 The right frame of mind (*understand your brain to understand how to study*)
2 Assignments – substance and style (*sending signposts of quality to a marker*)
3 Exams – agony and ecstasy (*riding the assessment roller coaster*)
4 Reports (*when an essay won't do*)
5 Referencing (*neglect this at your peril*)

1 THE RIGHT FRAME OF MIND

Remember, you only remember until you forget, but once you know, you know forever

First, in good academic style, there is always theory behind the practice. To know why study is hard can help tell us how it doesn't have to be. There is no right or wrong way to study, but there are some basic guidelines that can help make it more effective. There can be no rules, we are all different and some people just discover what works for them. Ultimately, it's all *in the mind* but commanding your curriculum is natural when you connect to its consequences. In other words, seeing how the content of study is relevant to you helps make study less difficult, and the results last longer.

Study can be so boring!

Few students like being assessed or revising for exams. So, how do you *tune* your brain to study and make it work harder? If you see the relevance of this question you are halfway to the answer. Partly, it's about seeing the relevance of something to you – the resulting *positive attitude* means you can study at a *higher altitude*.

Why does study hurt?

When you understand the 'cause' a solution is easier to find. So, why is study tough? It's tough because we are human, not because we are stupid. Neuroscientists will tell you the brain is a fabulous and complex organ. We are lucky, we all have one. To make the most of yours it helps to understand how it tries to help you. Importantly, the brain can be a greedy beast; perhaps a third of the energy we need to stay alive may be consumed running the brain when it is in a high performance mode. Study is a high performance mode – the brain has to do lots of work to grow.

Evolution would hardly have permitted human survival if people wasted precious energy, so we have adapted to conserve it whenever we can. When energy sources are plentiful some of us will see this conservation in our expanding waistbands – it's a body's way of preparing for periods when it might have to go hungry. We cannot help trying to conserve energy. This is why it can take an effort of will to do exercise, including mental exercise. The brain is clever in lots of ways. One way is how it saves energy by cutting down on the need to assess the environment, and the need to plan a reaction to it. It does this by categorizing familiar things and by developing some routines or habits to deal with choices. Just think of how we play tennis or drive a car.

Not everything we encounter will be familiar – 'Oh no, the house is on fire – RUN'. When we sense physical danger we can find bags of energy, it is what psychologists call the *flight and fight* response. Our sense of danger tells glands to flood the hormone, adrenaline, into our blood supply which helps release energy within our muscles quickly. This burst of energy helps us move rapidly to improve our survival chances. Before you think that frightening yourself will make your brain work harder, this response also diverts blood and energy away from the brain. This is because our body makes physical survival a priority, evolution tells us there is little benefit in having great processing capacity if you are dead. We see this reaction when people become hot-headed and lose their temper – the flight and fight response means people may act in ways they later regret because, at the time, their brain is not in its most rational mode – like a computer working in safe mode, there is less processing power available.

So, what has the 'fight and flight' response got to do with revision?

A bit of adrenaline probably helps in exam conditions. When we study, though, we need to have the brain working in a high performance mode, flooded with energy, but our natural instinct is to conserve energy. Why would your brain want to work this hard? It often doesn't, so study can feel tough but it does not have to.

Given adequate time and a calm emotional state to study, what is *the secret* of releasing the capacity of the brain and the energy needed to study?

Part of the answer is simple, we need to help the brain give up its conservation habit when we study. This is not as hard as it sounds. Think about the times when the brain slips into its high performance mode naturally – it does this when it is potentially useful to you. In other words, like flight and fight response for your muscles, your body releases bags of energy to the brain when it recognizes the need. For example, if you are making a risky or expensive purchase or when you are on a first date you may find your focal attention is quite sharp. This heightened sense of awareness comes from processing lots of new information. You can do this because you sense the priority for you, so the brain adopts a high performance processing mode. In other words, with the right motivation we find the energy to do things naturally, and with little effort.

Similarly, when we study it is important to be motivated *by the content* of the study, rather than just the result we want from an exam or assignment. Some of us may be motivated by wanting better jobs and maybe a qualification will help. However, qualification is a by-product of passing an exam – even if it might make someone more willing to study in the first place. The thing that will make a student more effective in exams is to be more engaged with the study materials in the first place.

For once, it is all about you

To take away the boredom and sharpen the mental appetite for study, the secret is to relate to the material, *connecting to its consequences*. If you see how it is important to *you* and to your understanding of *your world* then your brain will believe you need this information. It is natural to find the energy to deal with things which are important enough to us, as long as we recognize this importance. The secret is to make the brain connect with the relevance to you of what is being studied. You need to help it see how each topic of study relates to helping *you* navigate through relevant and potentially important choices that apply to *you*.

How? This means relating whatever you are reading or studying to your own experience. Try to recognize events in your own life and aspects of your world

153

that can be related to the topics you study. For example, how well does a business concept or communication model apply to your own experiences? Even if you have never been in business, we are all on the receiving end of promotional messages so this can be quite easy to do. This will help you see how these ideas can tell you something about the world *you* need to survive in. In other words – find your own examples, from your own experience, because this information *helps* you – it is not just something you have to read and remember. The more you can relate to an idea the easier it is to absorb and understand – and it feels natural.

Remember, you only remember until you forget, but once you know you know forever. If you understand why connecting with the ideas you are studying is important then you know how to study more effectively. Of course, it still helps to have some tricks to trigger this knowledge, particularly in situations like examinations, as section 3 explains.

Be gentle with yourself

A few words of warning though, we are not machines. With the high number of assessments and exams people take in their lives now, most people will be familiar with the experience of revising but wondering what happened to the last few minutes, *'I'm not taking anything in, I can't recall what I just read'*. Of course, it is hard to concentrate sometimes. For example, when we are tired, or unwell, or have distractions, or when we are emotionally upset. When such things are serious or out of our control it is useful to consider discussing them with tutors – to see if an extension is appropriate or if a plea for mitigating circumstances should be made.

When concentration does not come easily but problems are less serious most of us can take a break: perhaps have a coffee, go for a walk or have an early night. This can boost personal morale – which is important when studying. Sticking *at it* may make someone feel virtuous but when nothing is *going in* it can be a poor use of time and cause damage to self-confidence. Also, we often need time to reflect on what we are studying, particularly as we may have to *manipulate it* in our own thoughts – what examiners often call *critical thinking*. Because we all need time like this we need to allow for it when we plan to study. Try not to create extra pressures by finding you have too little time to study the material you need to cover. Most of us work well with some form of deadline but too much pressure can cause panic and stir up emotions that will interfere with the rational concentration needed to study well.

Like a good marketer

Like a professional marketing communicator, know where you are coming from and where you are trying to go; strategic marketers call this *analysis* and *planning*. This can apply to study as well as markets. Analysis of your situation will reveal the key pressures you have to balance: work, family and friends, domestic chores and study, etc. Time is precious for most of us nowadays, so identifying when it is most feasible to study is important. An analysis of your own study skills, and of the study tasks needed to pass is also valuable. Then you can identify and assess your options, to work out a range of plans that may achieve your desired goals. Which is best for you will require an honest assessment of your range of other commitments, finding spaces between these that are realistic – and sticking to your regime. How much study time can you find in a week and where? Do you need some other skills first, typing, filing, or speed reading, for example?

No one can study everything, so identifying key priorities will help you set aside times to study particular topics, and it is wise to balance the time devoted with any weighting given in a syllabus. It can help to identify different sets of priorities, so you can focus your time as deadlines approach. Deciding what are *must know*, *should know*, and 'nice to know' topic areas will give you a focus on the most important things you need to do. You can always return to the *nice to know* things when you are ahead of schedule. If you are behind schedule and have not covered *must know* things it will be easier to reschedule your study plan toward vital topics.

Planning, then, involves selecting your topics for study and keeping your morale up – if you find some areas easy do not put them to one side – they help your enthusiasm and give you confidence. Planning should also give you some rewards, try to mark your achievements with small treats and you will feel you are making real progress.

Taking notes

It can be daunting to return to material you have read before only to find you cannot recall what it said. It is valuable therefore to make notes as you go – and to take *ownership* of the material you read. If it is vital stuff, try photocopying it (unless you own it already) and write notes in margins as you go. Then, at natural breaks, try jotting down the key points together with your thoughts and observations. It will feel like you have captured the essence of what was there, and if you make clear and organized summaries of your notes these will act like a key into your memory, to bring the material to the front of your mind again.

The first time you read something, try to study in sections, e.g. whole sentences, paragraphs, or sub-sections, rather than dwelling on each word. The aim is to grasp the meaning of what is said, not to recall every word. If you dwell too long you will find it hard to follow the thread of an argument. Try to skip through sentences by using a pencil but only stop on the main words. For example, take that sentence again and focus on the words in bold: 'Try to **skip**

155

through **sentences** by using a **pencil** that only **stops** on the **main words**'. It sounds strange but most of us take in more if we read that bit faster. Try it – it takes a bit of practice but it can speed up your study (after a while you may find you are doing it without the pencil).

Organization

Effective study and revision takes some organization. Few of us can turn concentration on and off like a tap. Organize all the relevant materials you need – and keep them in order, grouped by topic. Consider using boxes or shelves to keep them together in relevant groups. Organize your own notes in relation to these groups – and keep a list of what is in each group (maybe keep a catalogue file if you have lots of different material). Your notes should act as a key into what is in each collection. If your notes get out of hand, then make notes of your notes. Above all, make your notes work for you. Good notes will trigger what you know without you having to re-study material. Try to make them manageable in size, aim for a one-page note that covers a key topic area, and try to make them memorable. You can do this by condensing notes down with tricks that highlight key issues – try using colours and drawing mind maps of key issues (like a scatter plan). The objective is to own the content of what the notes signify. By drawing diagrams and mind maps you will collect your ideas inside your head – so when you see the diagram it will trigger you to recall your understanding.

Study tips – summary

- Identify with the material you study – use examples from your own life.
- Set priorities for study materials – identify the
  - *** *must know*,
  - ** *should know*, and
  - * *nice to know* stuff.
- Set a timetable for study and match this to the range of areas to cover (allow for breaks and reflection, and if you slip behind focus on the *must know*).
- Read with purpose and in sections, keep the flow going using a pencil or pointer to guide your eyes to the key words.
- Make notes of the key issues and ideas (don't be afraid to mark study materials, if you own them).
- Organize your study materials so you can find them easily and keep a summary, in note form, of each section.

2 ASSIGNMENTS – SUBSTANCE AND STYLE

Imagine trying to mark something written like this:

> Alot of it's contents may look well riten .Noone minds thee odd tipo But and two besure your reedy too hand inn, tri too ask a fiend four there help two be sur.

Tutors are only human (yes, it is true) and making the most of them takes some understanding. Education is about students, of course, and study is about personal development. So, why be concerned about tutors? For a start, they are often markers too, so they know what is needed to pass. Personal development has its own rewards but having it recognized is usually part of a formal assessment that has to satisfy specific and carefully described outcomes. It is how we earn qualifications that people can trust. If you have a clear idea of what markers are looking for then you are far more likely to be able to provide this. If you are not, you should ask tutors to help, but do some reading on your own first if you want their respect and useful assistance.

Most programmes of study are accompanied by materials that try to explain what is expected of students. A student may not have a clear idea where a course is leading at the outset or what standards are expected from the assessments. Badgering a tutor is no substitute for personal scholarship, so explore course documents thoroughly before you approach him or her for more guidance, otherwise he or she may think you are lazy or dull. You are likely to have a more constructive discussion with a tutor if you have also prepared questions and identified specific issues. Just saying you don't understand a question is usually a sign of poor scholarship to a tutor – help will often be more generous when it is clear a student has already made some personal effort.

Style and depth – if you are not sure, don't guess

Study the syllabus and the learning outcomes to appreciate the ground you need to cover to pass, and the form and style that is often required. Normally, the type of outputs students must demonstrate in assessments will be described in course documents. Sometimes the scope of the study area will be prescribed with a *syllabus*, while the depth of the approach may appear in a list, sometimes called *learning outcomes* (or *learning objectives*).

Most modern programmes now try to cover the skills and type of knowledge students will be required to demonstrate. It is useful to reflect on what these might mean and to look at examples of successful work from previous assessments (if these are available). For example, introductory courses often seek to have students recognize and be able to describe core concepts. Intermediate courses often expect students to demonstrate an ability to apply core concepts and models. Higher level courses, and especially postgraduate courses, usually require critical thinking and a critical awareness of up-to-date thinking. This book is aimed at the latter two levels.

Often work must be presented in an academic style: that is, in a relatively objective style, where ideas and arguments are reasoned with clear logical debate and acknowledgement of the literature is provided. In such a case, care should be taken to avoid subjective personal opinion and it is rare to use first person pronouns, such as 'I'. Invariably, third person language works best in assignments. However, in business areas like marketing communications, there will be times when you are asked to present information in a professional style – perhaps in a business report, memo, or board briefing. This is more often the case in courses with vocational and professional content but can also apply elsewhere. In a business report, more emphasis may be placed on *applied* rather than *theoretical* content, but this is usually a matter of balance rather than alternatives. The character of presentation may also be less rigid than when using academic conventions but the reliability of the assignment will still depend on the authority of the original data and the strength of the reasoning – which is likely to be based on appropriate theory.

Have a heart for the marker, or she may break yours

If you think study can be awful, try to imagine what marking is like! You may suspect some of your fellow students do not write well and that some have scattered and ill-disciplined ideas. You will almost certainly be right. The people who will see this most clearly are likely to be those who will be asked to assess the work you and your colleagues produce. Of course there are model students. Try to imagine, though, how the marker will deal with perhaps dozens of scripts on a similar topic. What type of concentration and patience will he or she need? They may have to cope with scripts that contain *confused ideas*, presented using *poorly constructed sentences*, in documents with *incoherent structure*.

On top of this, tutors may feel disappointed if their efforts to explain things have been wasted and that some students have made little effort, even with basic referencing. Then, to cap it all, perhaps one student has included something from the Internet but was not sure how to reference it, and then 'forgot' to. So the marker has to *waste* twenty minutes tracking it down, and then has to write a report to raise the charge of high academic crime, 'plagiarism'. Try to imagine that your script is next, number twenty-five out of fifty-four in a pile. The marker has been going for two hours and twenty minutes when she reaches yours, one more and she will stop for a break . . . are you going to have a fair appraisal?

158

Most of us think our work is at least passable when we hand it in. Sometimes it is returned with a grade lower than hoped for. Is it injustice? We all hope markers are objective, and exam boards, colleges, professional bodies, and universities all employ systems to try to ensure fairness. Nevertheless, there are mistakes. Often, markers work with discretionary grading bands too, so some scripts will be at the bottom end of a band even when the marking is fine. Markers tend to be more forgiving in exam conditions, but for coursework, good presentation of a script is vital if you want to load the odds in your favour and avoid the risk of rough justice or being bottom of the grade band. Certainly, in a day where every computer has access to spell and grammar checks, there is really no need for obvious mistakes but do not rely on these alone.

Clarity and style

Those who re-read their submitted work later without finding confusing passages or errors are rare. Those who have never looked back through work at all will never know, which perhaps is more worrying. Confused ideas, incoherent structure and poorly constructed sentences will mean the grade will tumble downwards, undervaluing much of the reading and research effort behind the script (assuming such reading has been done).

If you think clarity and style do not matter then you are simply wrong, and you are putting great faith in a marker if you expect him or her to have the patience to work out what you are trying to say if it is not obvious. Imagine:

Script number twenty-five . . . fifteen minutes to a tea break, just do this one quickly first . . . then I'm nearly half way through the pile.

Improve your odds

Always try to complete a good draft of your work well enough in advance to be able to come back and read it at least once with fresh eyes. At the very least, leave it overnight and read it again carefully to correct errors before handing it in. Even a very good student makes errors; journalists need sub-editors to spot these things and even great authors need proofreaders. If you are working in a second language, find a good friend with stronger language skills than yours and ask her to proof your work. We may use our eyes to read but we see with our minds – when you have just written something and read it back it is easy to miss mistakes, because you see what you meant to say rather than what the markers will see when they read it.

So what should you do?

Here is a list of things that are common-sense when you do them, and daft when you don't:

- Read the question carefully – because many people don't.
- Know exactly what style you need to write in – and stick to it.
- In academic mode of address, avoid use of first person pronouns (I and me).
- Plan the structure at the outset – it will save time and clear your thoughts.
- Ensure your structure will be clear to a reader; consider using subheadings.
- Give clear signposts to the marker where you are taking her or him – briefly try to tell the marker what is coming, where, in what order and why.
- Consider putting linkages between key sections – like sentences that explain the relevance to the last section – or questions posed at the end of a section that will be answered or addressed in the next section.
- Consider topping and tailing the work – perhaps something like an abstract or an opening paragraph given at the outset, to explain what the benefit of reading this will be, and a summary at the end listing conclusions or findings.
- Only use quotations sparingly; it is very rare that they should be more than a couple of sentences long.
- Avoid offering factual data without evidence of the source, and reference all concepts and models introduced by using respected sources wherever possible.
- Use diagrams and tables to make points better than can be made in prose, and never to just duplicate or provide padding.
- Always give diagrams and tables a title and label all the important parts; provide a reference for the diagram if appropriate (do not expect the reader to hunt for it in the prose if it was mentioned in the text).
- Where a table or diagram is partly a student's own work but also draws on another existing published diagram, this should be acknowledged as adapted from the original author.
- When you have the bulk of the script in a good structure, consider if you can give your work an interest point at the outset – a hook to capture the reader's attention.
- Adopt a consistent referencing convention – the Harvard style often works best – and stick to it.

- Keep a list of things you often do wrong – typing errors or words you get confused over – then check these in your script.
- Read it with fresh eyes a day or two later and correct any errors.

Content is key

What the markers are looking for will be specific to an assignment, module, or course. Therefore, any points of advice can only be general guidelines. Typically, the marker is looking for evidence of the author being a *thinking machine* in the context of the question set and that she or he can present these thoughts in the style of accepted conventions of presentation.

In the context of the question, markers expect a student to provide evidence of understanding appropriate topics (theory, concepts, models, and relevant key issues). Normally, students will need to draw on academic sources that describe and evaluate these topics and the sources should be referenced and acknowledged clearly. These sources should also be well respected; just because something is 'published' on the Internet does not give it respect. Refereed journal articles, relevant industrial publications, and good textbooks are acceptable in most cases. Students who widen their reading beyond a core textbook and deal with current publications will normally gain extra credit, especially at higher levels of study. Above the most basic level of study, the uncritical reproduction of textbook material is rarely sufficient to pass an assessment (a photocopier can do this more efficiently).

Normally, a marker will expect to see evidence of understanding and reflection, demonstrated in your own words but drawing on ideas included and referenced found in the literature. Using original examples to illustrate ideas and concepts can show to the marker levels of critical thinking and a level of internalized understanding that will often gain extra credit. However, using clichéd examples from a textbook does not. Academic work should seek to avoid offering first hand subjective opinions in the development of any critical evaluations. Instead, conclusions should be debated and reasoned to show a disciplined thinking process. Credit will often be given for comparing and contrasting theories so as to illustrate their respective weakness or strengths. Remember also to try to illustrate the application of theory and ideas – as the real goal of academic argument is to reveal some truths about the wider world.

Disaster

Getting the question wrong is quite common. This may seem like too basic a piece of advice to be worth giving – but many students fail to take it. Some students jump at a key word and gallop off in the wrong direction. Others confuse words and see them as referring to a different issue. Some may read a quotation

161

and ignore the question set beneath it. Some take elements mentioned in a question and look them up on the Intranet, then paraphrase whatever they find, while taking little note of what is really being asked. Whatever the cause, failure to read a question carefully enough to understand what is being asked means that a student will be unlikely to address the relevant key issues appropriately. The marker will see this as a student failing to demonstrate understanding. No matter how good the critical thinking demonstrated, to answer a different question to the one set is to follow a recipe for disaster.

In general terms, in the context of the question set, markers are looking for opportunities to give credit for evidence of sound reasoning which draws on relevant academic concepts and contemporary reading. At higher levels of study, evidence of a critical appreciation of relevant contemporary academic content is essential. 'Critical' means exploring the value and relevance of whatever data, ideas, and issues are introduced, to show the ability to think and make assessments about them, and not to just accept them. Typically a student might try to show critical thinking by identifying shortcomings or strengths in academic models, theoretical constructs, or concepts. Normally, this will be done through sound reasoning and often by comparison with other models and concepts. Sometimes it will be done through illustrative use of the applied value of a model or concept, where its usefulness in practice can show a level of critical appreciation (again, this is one reason to offer examples).

Any unsupported assertions, such as claims of a factual style about a state of affairs, will lose credit in a script. These must be supported with evidence, either by offering clear attribution or else supported with original empirical evidence, sound reasoning or a combination of these. To do otherwise is to offer a subjective personal opinion. This is fine in a letter to a friend but is not an appropriate style for academic scripts, nor for any business document whose value will need to be assessed if management judgements are to be based on it. Academic scripts are trying to be relatively objective and to be *explicit* about this level of relative objectivity – so a reader can make a reasoned judgement about the worth of the content (rather than make a judgement about the author).

EXAMPLE

An example, dealing with a question directed at MBA students. Note, this is deliberately not in the area of integrated marketing communications, but is provided as an illustration of points previously made in this appendix.

You have been brought in as a marketing consultant to give advice to senior management. They tell you their main product is losing market share despite

its good value. They require you to produce a report that offers advice on the steps needed to select and implement a positioning strategy (include discussion on the practical difficulties that might be anticipated in managing this).

Notice that this question requests a report style. To answer this question by developing a strategy is wrong, this would not address the key issues asked about – the management steps in relation to a particular task and the issues to consider when implementing a plan. To suggest a strategy would be writing fiction and this would fail to deal with the need to be objective, there is no data to assess the relevant options to develop a strategy, so to develop one is to make it up, not to reason it.

The question here is seeking a critical understanding of the concept of strategic positioning and (specifically for MBA students, with their management experience) whether the candidate can critically consider the functional challenges for marketing of managing the efforts to bring about such a strategic outcome. A good answer would seek to define what a positioning strategy is, drawing on referenced sources, and would ideally explain some of the abstract issues and potential problems involved with identifying current position and dealing with the management of a current or desired position.

To do this, the concept of **positioning** and of what a **strategic goal** might be would both need to be clearly appreciated and explained in the script. That is, these issues would need to be critically considered. A discussion of the steps involved in this management process would also be appropriate, dealing with the information needed and how it can be gathered; and dealing with the modelling of the information with appropriate concepts and tools, to make sense of it (i.e. a critical exploration of some useful and appropriate tools). Within this, a sound answer would cover the rationale for having and managing a positioning strategy, and explain the importance for helping to manage the sense of relationship with a clearly defined set of stakeholders.

The work should also have included a discussion on the possible role, and challenges within this role, of managing the sort of proposition that a position strategy is seeking to support. Across a cohort of students, weak students are likely to do no more than list, in an uncritical way, a set of basic marketing planning steps. Other weak students are likely to carry out things like a SWOT analysis, and then try to offer strategic advice based on this. Both would be wrong.

Below is a guide to what a marker would expect at MBA level (Note: each school will have its own range of grades or marks in terms of pass/fail/merit, etc. These are just a guide):

19% and below **Serious fail**, inadequate identification of relevant academic content and failing to address a question.

20–29% **Poor fail**, weak descriptions of relevant material but with no evidence of applied thinking or any synthesis of conceptual material or any clearly demonstrated critical reasoning relevant to the question.

163

30–44%	**Fail**, mainly descriptive content with weak evidence of an adequate depth of comprehension. This will likely include paraphrased textbook material, with weak academic references and poor evidence of critical reasoning (with appropriate theory and academic constructs not clearly applied or critically explored).
45–49%	**Marginal fail**, often does contain evidence of some analytical thinking and reference to a body of appropriate academic literature. The work may attempt to draw on relevant key concepts, appropriately recognized, but often described without critical interpretation. The use of these concepts does not help fully address the question set and there may be little evidence of an understanding of the value of the application of models to business contexts.
50–59%	**Basic pass**, offers a level of interpretation based on current practice and relevant theoretical constructs along with industry activity, together with sound analysis that reveals some critical reasoning in relation to relevant academic material.
60–69%	**Good pass**, will critically explore the value of descriptive elements with the use of appropriate theoretical constructs, which are critically appraised for their interpretative value within a context of a transparent level of objectivity. Typically, concepts and theoretical constructs are used to evaluate documentary material and these are applied to contemporary issues and business practice, where relevant.
70% +	**Distinction level pass**, will combine all the above with critical insight and display evidence of deep levels of understanding.

3 EXAMS – AGONY AND ECSTASY

Sitting exams is not all agony – when they are done they are done – and when you get a great grade it can be very exciting. How to get that grade is something you should consider planning for.

Even if you have bags of time, when revising it can be important not to spend too long before taking a break. About thirty minutes is the optimum for most people to spend in hard concentration before taking a short break – and five minutes off should be enough. Such breaks allow time for reflection and it is also something to look forward to when you are covering a lot of revision quite quickly.

The value of note-taking is difficult to over emphasize when you revise. You will not remember everything and you will not have confidence you can recall things unless you jot down things to prompt you later. When you hit points you have not fully understood, include these in your notes to check out later rather than spend excessive time on them which will break your concentration and flow – that is unless these points are critical to what you are revising. Checking them out at the time will slow you down and interrupt your overall grasp of what you are revising.

Exams are not like real life – you cannot usually refer to stored information, usually you have to show you can recall and understand things, so a few memory tricks can be useful. Attitude and organization will help too. There is some evidence that the best way to revise is to use the formula below:

- First skim the section you are about to study – get a feel for the scale of what you are about to study – so it will not seem like an endless task. As you study you will have a feel for the progress you are making.
- Then jot down some of the key questions the section or chapter is about to deal with – so you have a clear map in your head of why this is important (e.g. why do we use integrated marketing communications, and how can it be applied?).
- Then *read, reflect, recite*, and *review*. *Read* the section (taking notes) – then *reflect* on and think about how your reading and notes answer the questions you mapped out. *Recite* and rehearse the answers to yourself in your own words – then you own the understanding, and your notes will trigger this. You only need to revise your notes then. Lastly *review* the whole chapter again – checking for things you have missed out.

Memory is important in most exams. So part of the revision process is about collecting ideas together in a way that means you can recall them easily later. One way to do this is to collect the ideas into groups. Few of us are good at recalling long lists of different information but if we can put these into families then the task becomes much easier. If you have a large family and are asked to list all your cousins it can be tough – but if you follow a family tree in your mind then it becomes much easier (e.g. my mother has two sisters and two brothers, John and James – James has been married twice and had two daughters with his first wife – Sue and Jane – and has one with his new wife – Mary, etc.). The idea is to do the same with your revision. You will likely know a long list of items but to recall what you know, in an orderly fashion, you will find a grouping structure useful. For example, if you want to list the cities in your country it can be much easier to break the country down into regions first and try to think of all the cities in each region. Have a go. Another classical memory trick is to use a *mnemonic*. This is a device, like a word or a saying that is easy to remember but has elements that stand for what you want to remember. One famous example refers to remembering the colours of the spectrum by taking the first letters of each colour and using these as the first letter of words in a sentence: 'Richard Of York Gave Battle In Vain' – ROYGBIV (red, orange, yellow, green, blue, indigo, violet).

Because, sometimes, it can be easier to remember an image or a place, it can be a useful devise to link information with your visual memory. Try taking something you are familiar with, like your bedroom, and associate different items you want to recall with elements in the place you are already familiar with. If you want to recall the people in your class you can identify them as sitting in a different part of the room – John and Shirley on the bed – Dan next to the door – Mary playing with the light switch, etc. If you draw a map of your room then you will think about who is in each different place.

One of the most common causes of examination failure is that students simply do not answer the set questions. Some students seem determined to give a potted version of their notes instead of attempting to apply their knowledge to the question itself. If questions are purely descriptive, then this should pose less of a problem, but for programmes at higher levels of study an examination is more likely to set questions that are more conceptually based, and the student will be expected to apply skills of understanding, analysis and reasoning. So not to answer the question set can be a disaster.

Question the question

In most exam situations, questions fall into two different styles: *descriptive* and *analytical*. Both types of question require the student to demonstrate that the question has been fully comprehended, but they often suggest a different style of approach in the way to answer them.

Descriptive questions usually begin with 'explain', 'define', 'outline', 'state', or 'describe'. To answer these types of questions a student will need to include explanations and definitions. Good answers will also usually include hypothetical or practical examples to reinforce the points made.

Analytical questions can be more difficult to answer. They usually begin with 'analyse', 'criticize', 'assess', 'evaluate', or 'discuss'. For this type of question it is usually important to put forward differing viewpoints and to try to support these viewpoints with appropriate examples. This will show an awareness of criticisms that can be levelled at particular viewpoints. Such an answer should end with a conclusion that summarizes the key issues and this presents an opportunity for the students to suggest a viewpoint or judgement about the balance of arguments related to the subject area in the question. A reasoned opinion will normally win credit – while an unsupported opinion will not.

Careful revision and preparation will help reduce 'nerves' that might be present before an examination. Try to follow the advice given in this Appendix.

Preparation

Practice will help in the lead up to the exam. If you can, find some past questions – or else set your own. Try to do these and it will give you a feel for how long you have. This will also build confidence – particularly if you can compare your attempt, and the indicative answers available. If there are such answers, try to do the question blind, then compare what you have left out. Compare the answer with your notes too. Are they relatively complete? For those who cannot force themselves to set their own mock exam it is still a very useful thing to plan and sketch what answer you would give to a question. This forces you to start planning your answers, which can make a much more polished response possible in the exam proper. It also gives you a chance to see if you are missing things out when you compare the sketch to textbooks and model answers. That way you know if your revision is being effective.

The big day

Read instructions about what you can take into the venue, collect these together and check them the night before. If you do not know the venue allow plenty of time to find it. Even if you know it, always allow extra time on the day in case of hold-ups on the way. You don't want to start in a state of panic because you are late or because you had to abandon a car on yellow lines.

During the exam read and re-read all instructions and questions carefully. It helps to rate questions in terms of whether they can be answered adequately. Then a choice can be made effectively. It should then be possible to list the order in which the selected questions are to be answered. It may be best to start with the one where the subject-matter is best known; this will build up self-confidence to attempt what may seem to be the more difficult questions later.

After thinking about which questions to answer, prepare an essay plan consisting of brief notes made at the beginning of the answer book, giving the main points and structure of the essay. Jot down your mnemonics if you have any. Having a plan gives direction to an answer, making it easier to compose. It is better to start the actual answer on a new page and, when the answer is finished, lightly cross out the essay plan. Other obvious points are to write legibly and to number all answers correctly and clearly, making sure that additional sheets have your name or number on them and these are attached to the answer book in chronological sequence.

Budget your time in order to complete the number of questions to be attempted; this normally means, when marks are equal, spending equal time on each answer. When papers are sectionalized with disproportionate marks, pay particular attention to the mark apportionment and the guidelines given. Remember that time is at a premium, so do not waste it by repeating the examination question or the same words or phrases.

When you write an answer, use your plan. Tick off the key points you are covering and if you think of new ones, do not rely on holding them in mind, instead jot them down in your plan. Allow enough time to return to the answer and read it through at the end. You will almost certainly find you have some confused passages or some sentences that make little sense. Remember that the marker will not spend long on this script so try to make it easy for him or her to spot what you have worked hard to revise. Layout and white space can be very valuable. Also, consider highlighting or underlining key words or issues so they stand out quickly. If you use a diagram it can save on time, provided it makes points or explains issues clearly. Do not repeat the same things in text though, this will duplicate things that will gain no extra credit and will waste time you could devote to more content.

Finally, remember to write enough; candidates often fail by giving only embryonic answers – you must give enough detail to demonstrate a depth of understanding and not just short term recall of a concept – so applications of concepts and examples of practice are often valuable. If you are told to write the number of the questions attempted on the front of an answer book then remember to do it, you don't want to put an examiner in a worse mood by having to do it for you.

4 REPORTS

Report purpose

Reports communicate ideas and share understanding. They are produced with a business objective in mind – to communicate ideas to a particular audience efficiently. There is no one style of report but common sense is a great asset in shaping one. This is a short report on what should be in a report, and how to build one.

Where to start

To start, try to answer the questions:

- Why is the report needed?
- Who is it for?
- How will they use it?
- What do they already know?
- When do they need it?

From this it should be possible to agree clear objectives (*what is the intended outcome?*), then to identify the core subject area, and to define the range and scope of information needed. It will help to write down a statement of the purpose for which the report is needed and return to this if the task starts to lose focus.

Report stages

There are several phases to constructing most reports.

First, **scope** the task to gain an understating of breadth of the topics and the scale of importance to the readership (who will use it and for what?). This will help identify the depth of research needed. It is often useful to look at older reports on related issues to see what structure these have given to the subject area. The critical thing is to understand why the report is needed and what decision may rest on it.

Second, **data collection** is needed to gather the relevant information. Sometimes this may involve commissioning or conducting original research but often it will mean bringing together already published data from different sources.

Third, **organization**, involves putting the collated material into a logical and user-friendly order. This should aim to give the document a clear and relevant structure for its task, so ideas are grouped together in order to build an understanding of the issues in a logical sequence. By putting information into sections with an order that gives a sense of progressive development, the final report will build toward a coherent document that gives a picture of the issues being reported on.

Fourth, **writing** the report takes the information gathered and presents it so that the information gathered becomes accessible and transparent – without jargon or unnecessary detail.

Finally, **proofing**, when you review and revise the document, to improve it and polish it.

'**SCOWP**' up the task:

Scope	S
Data **C**ollection	C
Organization	O
Writing	W
Proofing	P

Character of a report

Different reports will need different levels of detail but they all need to be of a quality fit for their task, when they are 'fit' they're powerful – like big '**CCATS**':

- **C** for **Clear** – to be understood easily.
- **C** for **Comprehensive** – all the essential relevant information.
- **A** for **Accurate** – relatively up-to-date and precise enough for the task.
- **T** for **Timely** – in the hands of those who need it in time for the tasks at hand.
- **S** for **Succinct** – contain needed information which is not lost in detail.

Report checklist

Use the report checklist shown on the facing page to structure your report.

Report layout

There is no such thing as a perfect report layout – it is a document designed to communicate – and communication is about craft and science, but a typical general report layout might start with these headings:

- Title page
- Executive summary
- Table of contents
- Introduction
- Methodology
- Findings
- Limitations
- Conclusions (recommendations)
- Appendices

Often, one of the key roles of a report is to be able to promote orderly discussion of key issues at meetings. Therefore, being able to identify key points in a document quickly is important. The use of headings and sub-headings can be valuable for this. In a long report it can also help to number the sections (e.g. 1.0, 1.1, 1.2; 2.0, 2.1, 2.2; 3.0, 3.1.i, 3.1.ii, 3.2, 3.3, etc.).

Report conclusions

Most reports will contain a summary of the main issue revealed. Sometimes they may also include recommendations, but this will usually be when they have been called for or when the character of the data suggests this will be potentially

A REPORT CHECK LIST

To write a good report:

- **Stick to the task**:
  Keep the objectives in sight – remember why a report is needed and state the objective in the report at an early stage to inform or remind a reader.

- **Avoid unnecessary technical detail** and boring content:
  Use an appendix if you must include some of this.

- **Use the language of the reader**:
  If there are professional terms commonly used then this is normally acceptable but do not talk down to or over the heads of your readers – effective communication of ideas and understanding is the goal.

- **Polish the prose**:
  Don't say – 'statistical analysis of the variables produces a significant correlation between the third and fifth item', do say – 'prices charged and the level of sales are closely linked'.

- **Organize** the report layout:
  E.g. Title page, with topic, target, date, author, etc., and an Executive summary, with explanation of the heart of the report and the confidence of outcomes, etc., see following 'report layout' for a list of headings.

- **Use diagrams**, graphs, and tables to clarify and explain:
  It is often much easier to understand a table than a paragraph of data, for example:

  The number of undergraduates awarded first-class degrees since 2000, includes: the 2000 figure of 56 (4%), the 2001 figure of 59 (4.5%), the 2002 figure of 63 (4.8%), the 2003 figure of 55 (3.5%) and the 2004 figure of 54 (3.4%).

  The number of undergraduates at UXY awarded first-class degrees since 2000

Year	Students	Percentage of graduates
2000	56	(4)
2001	59	(4.5)
2002	63	(4.8)
2003	55	(3.5)
2004	54	(3.4)

  (Base – students graduating from UXY, UXY figures in annual reports)

171

helpful. In business a report is often produced to support a decision-making process. In that sense it is not necessarily the case that a report needs to offer recommendations. The strength of such a report would be its character to help understand the relevant issues – then management can make an informed judgement.

5 REFERENCING

To a marker the standard of referencing is often a quick guide to the care a student has taken preparing a script. It certainly indicates a level of competency in academic presentation. Neglect it at your peril.

Clarity in communications and the ability to trace a source are the objectives of good referencing. There are several systems commonly used and students should be familiar with these from their own reading. Every textbook and academic journal provides examples of good practice. It is important to be consistent in each piece of work in how you reference. The way you reference may also need to follow a specific style or set of conventions depending on the guidelines for specific assessments.

If in doubt reference it. In an academic style of address, it is not acceptable to use unsupported assertions, or give factual claims or data without the source, and never describe theory or concepts without acknowledging the author in some way. The outcome of academic conventions and reference style should be to make you, the author of your script, relatively neutral in terms of the views portrayed within the assignment. It is not your opinions that are being put on the line; you are recanting the wisdom of others percolated from what should be respected, reputable and referenced sources.

This means your work will be relatively objective in that it is able to stand apart from any ownership related to factual statements about the world that you may use as assumption in the logic of any arguments you present about events. In this academic style, if someone wants to take issue with your work then they would need to take issue with the original sources you are quoting. If these sources are wrong then this is not something you can take the blame for. A reader may, though, take issue with you in terms of the choice of sources in the first place, or the character of your reasoning and the quality of your refer- encing. Poor referencing makes it difficult or impossible to trace the provenance of arguments you are putting forward – and if you do not reference the ideas of other people when you describe them then this is regarded as a serious academic crime – a form of 'passing off' which is viewed as a form of theft known as plagiarism.

Most work will need references

These are likely to be in the text in some form, and are also likely to be listed in more detail at the end of a section or end of a publication in a references list or bibliography or both. Sometimes the references in the text are nothing more than numbers that refer to the references list, but it is more common to ident-ify the author, and usually the year of publication of the referred to source, and, particularly when using a quotation, the page reference. The later full reference sections will normally contain complete details, perhaps including other authors or editors, and publication details like the journal or book title, volume or number, and the name and home city of the publisher.

References in the text

In some systems an author's name, publication date (and perhaps page reference) will be given in parentheses in the text (but when author and date are clear from the text, a page reference is enough), e.g.:

He was best known for his catch phrase, 'shut that door' (Smith 1999, 55).

When the author's name occurs in the sentence the reference consists of date (and perhaps page), e.g.:

Smith says he was best known for his catch phrase, 'shut that door' (1999, 55).

If there are two or more references these should be separated by semicolons: (Smith 1999; Knight and Day 2004). When work has more than three authors, only the first name is needed and this can be followed by '*et al.*', meaning 'and others'.

References at the end

When a list of references is given at the end it should include all work cited within a script. A short title system would use a bibliography which might include all materials used in preparing a script even if some of these are not referred to in the text. In this case a list might be placed at the end of the text, usually titled *References* or *List of References*.

For example, details listed in references for books:

Author/editor, date: Title. Edition (if relevant). Number of volumes (if relevant). Place: Publisher. e.g.:

Brown, M., Green J. and Blue. B. (eds.) (1999): Marketing at a crossroads. 3rd edn. 2 vols. London: LU Press.

(The surname of the first author will always be given first but subsequent authors may reverse the name order (J. Green).)

For example, details listed in references for articles:

1 Periodicals:

Author, Date: Title. Periodical, volume/issue number, inclusive page numbers.

2 Edited volumes:

Author, date: Title. In, editor (ed.), Title, place: publisher, inclusive page numbers.

Bibliography or References at the end

Sometimes there will be both a section with references as well as a bibliography. In most academic assignments a bibliography is a common requirement. It usually includes all items referred to in developing a script. In such a case this may be sufficient at the end of a piece of work without a separate references section. Items referenced in the text would then cross reference to the items in the bibliography – but there may be additional items not mentioned in the text. Students will gain little credit though for just collecting reading lists as a bibliography if there is no sign of the published material enriching the script. A bibliography should show sources arranged alphabetically (A–Z) by the surname (family name) of the authors. (When an author has several pieces of work cited, references should be ordered by date of publication, or alphabetically by title, or else indicated by a letter e.g. a, b, c, etc.)

Bibliography:

Mouse, M. and Pluto, D. (eds.), (1999) *The Story of Cartoons,* 3rd edn, New York: Fiction Press.

Snake, C., (1989) 'Look No Legs', in *The Zoo,* ed. B. Poster, London: Animal Press, pp. 23–26.

Short-title systems and the use of notes

For short-title systems references will usually be found in notes at the end of the scripts and within the text by something like a superscript number, e.g. Good idea[2].

174

With references in notes a full reference is usually given in the first use of the work, for example:

According to James Joyce,[1] 'Vicars don't all believe in God'.

Note:

1 Joyce, J. (2003), *A Guide to the Clergy of Liverpool* (Knowall Books, Bristol, 2003), p. 5.

The next time this is used a short form may be adopted just with the author's surname, title and page number (and sometimes the title may be shortened too):

4 Joyce, *A Guide to the Clergy*, p. 6.

Where reference is made to work just cited in an immediately preceding note, this can be referenced with 'ibid.'. This takes the place of the author's details and the work as much of it will be identical:

4 Joyce, *A Guide to the Clergy* . . ., p. 6.
5 Ibid.   (details as in preceding note)
6 Ibid., p. 8.   (details as in preceding note but different page)

Referencing books using notes:

Author, Title, Editor (if applicable), edition (if applicable), number of volumes (publisher, place of publication, date), volume number, page number.

The publisher may be omitted but the convention used must be consistent.

Referencing articles using notes:

1 Periodicals:
Author, Title, Periodical, volume/issue number (date), inclusive page numbers.

2 Edited volumes:
Author, Title, in *Title of book*, ed. Editor (publisher, place, date), inclusive pages.

Referencing and the Internet

Take care with the Internet. Many sources have little credibility. Just because they are accessible publicly does not make them reputable. Bibliographies are not easy on the Internet. The purpose of referencing is to make it possible for the reader to identify and trace the original material, so it can be examined in its own context. Because Internet sites come and go, have various levels of access and can be updated or changed, this becomes quite problematic.

Books

To cite a book accessed on the Internet you may need the author, title, and all the publication details of the sources, for example:

> Doe, J. *How to Make Money* (Internet). Hull (UK): Hull University Library, Electronic Text Centre, 1996; *c.*2000 (updated 1999, January; cited 2003, 3 November). 840K bytes. Available from http://hull.ac.uk/ul/hubs/public/doe.html

Newsprint

Newspapers may be cited, for example:

> Jones, John. Inflation never again. *Financial Times* (UK edition). 2003, 4 November, Business Section p. 2, (col. 2).

but to cite this taken from a website would be more complex:

> Jones, John. Inflation never again will this have the UK in fear. *Financial Times* (UK edn) [Internet]. 2003, 4 November [cited 2003, 4 November]: available from http://www.ft.com/uk/article &569956%%.html?mod=news%%ecomfusFUS%5
> Requires a subscription.

The Web

To cite a website:

> University of Hull Library Service, Homepage [Internet]. Author: Library Services: Hull University Library [updated 2003. 26 September 2003]. (cited 2003, 4 November). Available from http://www.hull.ac.uk/lib

 176

Bear in mind that the Internet is still relatively new and conventions for referencing are still quite fluid. If in doubt, return to basic principles and do all you can to make the sources traceable and your access to it transparent.

A few last few words of warning about the Internet – don't rely on it too heavily and never borrow from it without acknowledgement. Tutors are increasingly skilled at finding material available from the Internet, and search engines work to find material both for students and tutors. Many educational institutions now also employ specialist teams to examine scripts for plagiarism – so if in doubt about use of something, do reference it as best you can but do not ignore the issue.

Bibliography

1 Scene setting: theory and practice

De Pelsmacker, P., Geuens, M., and Van den Bergh, J. (2004), *Marketing Communications*, Financial Times/Prentice Hall: London.

Duncan, T. (2002), *IMC: Using Advertising and Promotion to Build Brands*, McGraw Hill: Boston, MA.

Kennedy, C. (2003), 'Cautionary Tales', *Director*, November: 62–68.

Kitchen, P.J. (1999), *Marketing Communications: Principles and Practice*, International Thomson: London.

Kitchen, P.J. (ed.) (2003), *The Rhetoric and Reality of Marketing: An International Managerial Approach*, Palgrave: Basingstoke.

Kitchen, P.J. and Schultz, D.E. (2001), *Raising the Corporate Umbrella: Corporate Communications in the Twenty-first Century*, Palgrave: Basingstoke.

Kitchen, P.J., Brignell, J., Li, T., and Spickett-Jones, J.G. (2004), 'The emergence of IMC: a literature review and critical commentary' in press for *Journal of Advertising Research*, forthcoming.

Schultz, D.E. (1993), 'Integrated marketing communications: maybe definition is in the point of view?', *Marketing News*, 18 January: 17.

Schultz, D.E. and Kitchen, P.J. (2000), *Communicating Globally: An Integrated Marketing Approach*, Palgrave: Basingstoke.

2 Integrated marketing communications

Caywood, C., Schultz, D.E., and Wang, P. (1991), 'Integrated Marketing Communications: a Survey of National Goods Advertisers', *unpublished report*, Medill School of Journalism, Northwestern University, June 1991.

Clow, K.E. and Baack, D. (2002), *Integrated Advertising, Promotion and Marketing Communications*, Pearson Education, Inc.: New Jersey.

De Pelsmacker, P., Geuens, M., and Van den Bergh, J. (2004), *Marketing Communications*, Financial Times/Prentice Hall: London.

Duncan, T. (2002), *IMC: Using Advertising and Promotion to Build Brands*, International Edition, The McGraw-Hill Companies, Inc.: New York.

Duncan, T.R. and Everett, S.E. (1993), 'Client perceptions of integrated communications', *Journal of Advertising Research*, 32, 3: 30–39.

Eagle, L.C. and Kitchen, P.J. (2000), 'IMC, brand communications, and corporate cultures: client/advertising agency co-ordination and cohesion', *European Journal of Marketing*, 34, 5/6: 667–686.

Fill, C. (1995), *Marketing Communications: Frameworks, Theories and Applications*, Prentice Hall International (UK) Limited: Hertfordshire.

Gould, S.J., Lerman, B., and Grein, A.F. (1999), 'Agency perceptions and practices on Global IMC', *Journal of Advertising Research*, 39, 1: 7–20.

Kaye, R.L. (1999), 'Companies need to realise internal marketing's potential', *Advertising Age's Business Review*, Chicago, 84, 7: 13.

Kitchen, P.J. (1999), *Marketing Communications: Principles And Practice*, International Thomson Business Press: London.

Kitchen, P.J. and Schultz, D.E. (1999), 'A multi-country comparison of the drive for IMC', *Journal of Advertising Research*, New York, 39, 1: 21–38.

Kitchen, P.J., Brignell, J., Li, T., and Spickett-Jones, J.G. (2004), 'The emergence of IMC: a literature review and critical commentary', *Journal of Advertising Research*, 44: 1.

Moriarty, S.E. (1994), 'PR and IMC: the benefits of integration', *Public Relations Quarterly*, Fall, vol. 39, 3: 38.

Pickton, D. and Broderick, A. (2001), *Integrated Marketing Communications*, Pearson Education Limited: Essex.

Schultz, D.E. (2000), 'Structural flaws dash marcom plans', *Marketing News*, Chicago, IL, vol. 34, 18: 9.

Schultz, D.E. (2001), 'Campaign approach shouldn't exist in IMC', *Marketing News*, Chicago, 35, 14: 8.

Schultz, D.E. and Kitchen, P.J. (2000), *Communicating Globally: an Integrated Marketing Approach*, Palgrave-Macmillan: London.

Schultz, D.E., Tannenbaum, S., and Lauterborn, R.L. (1993), *Integrated Marketing Communications*, NTC Business Books: Chicago.

Schultz, D.E. and Schultz, H. (2003), *IMC: the Next Generation*, McGraw Hill: New York.

Shimp, T.A. (2000), *Advertising Promotion: Supplemental Aspects of Integrated Marketing Communications*, 5th edn, The Dryden Press, Harcourt College Publishers: Fort Worth, TX, 19, 22, 29.

Sirgy, M.J. (1998), *Integrated Marketing Communications: A Systems Approach*, Prentice Hall: New York.

Smith, P.R. (2002), *Marketing Communications: An Integrated Approach*, 3rd edn, Kogan Page Limited: London, 4, 10, 17, 163.

Yeshin, T. (1998), *Marketing Communications Strategy 1998–99*, Butterworth-Heinemann: Oxford.

3 Advertising

Ambler, T. (2000), 'Persuasion, pride and prejudice: how ads work', *International Journal of Advertising*, 19, 3: 299–315.

Barnard, N. and Ehrenberg, A.S.C. (1997), 'Advertising: strongly persuasive or nudging?' *Journal of Advertising Research*, 37, 1: 21–31.

Barry, T.E. (1987), 'The development of the hierarchy of effects: a historical perspective', *Current Issues and Research In Advertising*, 10, 2: 251–295.

Barry, T.E. and Howard, D.J. (1990), 'A review and critique of the hierarchy of effects in advertising', *International Journal of Advertising*, 9, 2: 121–135.

Benham, L. (1972), 'The effect of advertising on the price of eyeglasses', *The Journal of Law and Economics*, 15, October: 337–352.

Berkman, H.W. and Gilson, C. (1987), *Advertising*, 2nd edn, Random House: New York.

Boyd, H.W. Jnr, Walker, O.C. Jnr, and Larreche, J.-C. (1998), *Marketing Management: A Strategic Approach with a Global Orientation*, McGraw Hill: London.

Buchholz, T.G. (2003), *Burger, Fries and Lawyers: The Beef Behind Obesity Lawsuits*. Available at US Chamber of Commerce and US Chamber Institute for Legal Reform website, www.uschamber.com (accessed 5 August 2003).

Bulmer, S.L. and Buchanan-Oliver, M. (2004), 'Meaningless or meaningful? interpretation and intentionality in post-modern communication', *Journal of Marketing Communication*, 10, 1: 1–16.

Calfee, J.E. and Ringold, D.J. (1994), 'The 70% majority: enduring consumer beliefs about advertising', *Journal of Public Policy and Marketing*, 13, 2: 228–238.

Churchill, G.A. and Peter, J.P. (1998), *Marketing. Creating Value for Customers*, 2nd edn, McGraw Hill: Boston, MA.

Denny, N. (1999), 'Advertisers attack FoE on kid's TV ads curfew', *Marketing*, 1 April: 7.

Eagle, L.C. and Kitchen, P.J. (2000), 'Building brands or bolstering egos? a comparative review of the impact and measurement of advertising on brand equity', *Journal of Marketing Communication*, 6, 2: 91–106.

Ehrenberg, A.S.C. (2001), 'Marketing: romantic or realistic?' *Journal of Advertising Research*, 40, 6: 39–48.

Ehrenberg, A.S.C., Barnard, N., and Scriven, J.A. (1997), 'Justifying our advertising budgets', *Marketing and Research Today*, 25, 1: 38–44.

Eisenberg, A.L. (1936), cited in Wartella, E.A. and Jennings, N. (2000), 'Children and computers: new technology – old concerns', *The Future of Children*, 10, 2: 31–43.

Ewing, M.T., De Bussy, N.M., and Caruana, A. (2000), 'Perceived agency politics and conflicts of interest as potential barriers to IMC orientation', *Journal of Marketing Communication*, 6, 107–119.

Flandin, M.P., Martin, E., and Simkin, L.P. (1992), 'Advertising effectiveness research: a survey of agencies, clients and conflicts', *International Journal of Advertising*, 11, 3: 203–214.

French, S.A., Story, M., and Jeffrey, R.W. (2001), 'Environmental influences on eating and physical activity', *Annual Review of Public Health*, 22: 309–335.

Heath, R. (2001), 'Low involvement processing – a new model of brand communication', *Journal of Marketing Communications*, 7, 1: 27–33.

Helgesen, T. (1996), 'The power of advertising – myths and realities', *Marketing and Research Today*, May: 63–71.

Hennessey, J. (1998), *Global Marketing Strategies*, 4th edn, Houghton Mifflin: Boston, MA.

Higham, N. (1999), 'Industry divided over prospect of ban on children's advertising', *Marketing Week*, 8, July: 17.

Jones, J.P. (1990), 'Advertising: strong force or weak force? Two views an ocean apart', *International Journal of Advertising*, 9, 3: 233–246.

Jung, C. and Seldon, B.J. (1995), 'The macroeconomic relation between advertising and consumption', *Southern Economic Journal*, 61, 3: 577–587.

Kirkpatrick, J. (1986), 'A philosophic defence of advertising', *The Journal of Advertising*, 15, 2: 42–50.

Kotabe, M. and Helsen, K. (1998), *Global Marketing Management*, John Wiley & Son: New York.

Kotler, P. (1980), *Principles of Marketing*, Prentice Hall: Englewood Cliffs, NJ.

Kotler, P. (2000), *Marketing Management* (millennium edn), Prentice-Hall Inc: Upper Saddle River, NJ.

Lannon, J. (1996), 'Integrated Communications from the Consumer End', *Admap*, February.

McCall, D. (1999), 'Plan to ban children's TV ads is an age-old mistake', *Marketing Week*, 2, September: 14.

McLellan, F. (2002), 'Marketing and advertising: harmful to children's health', *The Lancet*, 360, 9338: 1001.

Meyers-Levy, J. and Malaviya, P. (1999), 'Consumer processing of persuasive advertisements: an integrative framework of persuasion theories', *Journal of Marketing*, 63, 4: 45–60.

Perrault, W.D. and McCarthy, E.J. (1999), *Basic Marketing: a Global Managerial Approach*, McGraw Hill: Boston.

Preston, C. (2000), 'Are Children Seeing through ITC Regulations?' *International Journal of Advertising*, 19, 1: 117–136.

Shankar, A. (1999), 'Advertising's imbroglio', *Journal of Marketing Communications*, 5, 1: 1–15.

Shimp, T.A. (2003), *Advertising, Promotion, & Supplemental Aspects of Integrated Marketing Communications*, 6th edn, South-western/Thompson Learning: Mason Ohio.

Telser, L. (1964), 'Advertising and competition', *Journal of Political Economy*, 72, December: 547–551.

Weilbacher, W.M. (2001), 'Point of view: does advertising cause a "hierarchy of effects"?', *Journal of Advertising Research*, 41, 6: 19–26.

Young, B. and Webley, P. (1996), *The Role Of Television Advertising In Children's Food Choice*, Ministry of Agriculture, Fisheries and Food (MAFF): UK.

4 Sales promotion

Advertising Age, (2003), 23, March.

Bawa, K. and Srinivasan, S.S. (1997), 'Coupon attractiveness and coupon proneness: a framework for modelling coupon redemption', *Journal of Marketing Research*, 34, 4: 517–525.

Brassington, F. and Pettitt, S. (2003), *Principles of Marketing*, Financial Times Management.

Clow, K.E. and Baack, D. (2002), *Integrated Advertising, Promotion and Marketing Communications*, Prentice Hall/Pearson Education: Upper Saddle River, NJ.

D'Astous, A. and Jacobs, I. (2002), 'Understanding consumer reactions to premium-based promotional offers', *European Journal of Marketing*, 36, 11: 1270–1286.

De Pelsmacker, P. and Van den Bergh, J. (1998), 'Ad content, product category, campaign weight and irritation. A study of 226 TV commercials', *Journal of International Consumer Marketing*, 10, 4: 5–27.

De Pelsmacker, P., Geuens, M., and Van den Bergh, J. (2004), *Marketing Communications. A European Perspective*, Financial Times/Prentice Hall: Harlow.

Farris, P.W. and Ailawadi, K.L. (1992), 'Retail power: monster or mouse?', *Journal of Retailing*, Winter: 351–369.

Fill, C. (2002), *Marketing Communications. Contexts, Strategies and Applications*, Financial Times/Prentice Hall: Harlow.

Gardener, E. and Trivedi, M. (1998), 'A communication framework to evaluate sales promotion strategies', *Journal of Advertising Research*, 38, 3: 67–71.

Gupta, S. and Cooper, L. (1992), 'The discounting of discount and promotion brands', *Journal of Consumer Research*, 19, December: 401–411.

Inman, J.J. and Winer, R.S. (1998), *Where the rubber meets the road: a model of in-store consumer decision making*, Working Paper, report no. 98–122, Marketing Science Institute: Cambridge, MA.

Institute of Sales Promotion: www.isp.org.uk.

Jones, J.P. (1990), 'The double jeopardy of sales promotions', *Harvard Business Review*, September/October, 141–152.

Kasulis, J.J. (1999), 'Managing trade promotions in the context of market power', *Journal of the Academy of Marketing Science*, 27, 3: 320–332.

Kotler, P. (2003), *Marketing Management*, Prentice Hall: Upper Saddle River, NJ.

Lucas, A. (1996), 'In-store trade promotions', *Journal of Consumer Marketing*, 13, 2: 48–50.

NCH Marketing Services (2001), *UK Coupon Market 2000*.

O'Malley, L. (1998), 'Can loyalty schemes really build loyalty?', *Marketing Intelligence and Planning*, 16, 1: 47–55.

Ong, B.S. and Ho, F.N. (1997), 'Consumer perceptions of bonus packs: an exploratory analysis', *Journal of Consumer Marketing*, 14, 2–3: 102–112.

POPAI Europe (1998), *The POPAI Europe consumer buying habits study*, coordinated by Retail Marketing In-Store Services Ltd, Watford, Herts.: POPAI Europe.

5 Direct marketing

Brassington, F. and Pettitt, S. (2003), *Principles of Marketing*, Financial Times Management: London.

Clow, K.E. and Baack, D. (2002), *Integrated Advertising, Promotion and Marketing Communications*, Prentice Hall/Pearson Education: Upper Saddle River, NJ.

De Pelsmacker, P., Geuens, M., and Van den Bergh, J. (2004), *Marketing Communications. A European Perspective*, Financial Times/Prentice Hall: Harlow.

Direct Marketing Association (2000), *Statistical Fact Book '99*, Direct Marketing Association: New York.

Duncan, T. (2002), *IMC Using Advertising and Promotion to Build Brands*, McGraw Hill/Irwin: Boston, MA.

Evans, C.R. (1994), *Marketing Channels. Infomercials and the Future of Televised Marketing*, Prentice Hall: Englewood Cliffs, NJ.

FEDMA (2003a), *Best of Europe 2000/2001*, www.fedma.org, accessed 10 June 2003.

FEDMA (2003b), *Survey on Direct and Interactive Marketing Activities in Europe*, www.fedma.org (accessed 10 June 2003).

Fill, C. (2002), *Marketing Communications. Contexts, Strategies and Applications*, Financial Times/Prentice Hall: Harlow.

Kobs, J. (2001), *Profitable Direct Marketing. A Strategic Guide to Starting, Improving and Expanding Direct Marketing Operation*, McGraw-Hill/Contemporary Books: Chicago, IL.

Miles, L. (2001), 'Should DM still be missing its mark?', *Marketing*, 14, June: 29–31.

Picton, D.A. and Broderick, A. (2001), *Integrated Marketing Communications*, Prentice Hall: London.

Ridgeway, J. (2000), 'DirectWatch in 2000', *Marketing*, 21, December: 24–25.

Singh, S. (2001), 'Brands take the direct route', *Marketing Week*, 13 September, 38–39.

Stewart, D.W. (1996), 'Market-back approach to the design of integrated communication programs: a change in paradigm and a focus on determinants of success', *Journal of Business Research*, 37: 147–153.

Tapp, A. (2001), 'The strategic value of direct marketing: what are we good at?', *Journal of Database Marketing*, 9, 1: 9–15.

Verhoef, P., Hoekstra, J., and van Aalst, M. (2000), 'The effectiveness of direct response radio commercials. Results of a field experiment in The Netherlands', *European Journal of Marketing*, 34, 1/2: 143–155.

6 Marketing public relations

Berkman, H.W. and Gilson, C. (1987), *Advertising*, 2nd edn, Random House: New York.

De Pelsmacker, P., Geuens, M., and Van den Bergh, J. (2004), *Marketing Communications: A European Approach*, Pearson Education Ltd: Harlow.

Gronstedt, A. (1996), 'How agencies can support integrated communications', *Journal of Business Research*, 37, 201–206.

Harris, T.L. (1993a), *The Marketers Guide to Public Relations*, John Wiley & Sons: New York.

Harris, T.L. (1993b), 'How MPR adds value to integrated marketing communications', *Public Relations Quarterly*, Summer, 13–18.

Harris, T.L. (1998), *Value-Added Public Relations*, John Wiley & Sons: New York.

Kitchen, P.J. (1997), *Public Relations: Principles and Practice*, Thomson Learning: London.

Kitchen, P.J. (1999), *Marketing Communications: Principles and Practice*, Thomson Learning: London.

Kitchen, P.J. (2003), 'Why PR's skills at building relationships are vital in the new "Marketspace"' in *Behind the Spin*, College of St Mark and St John, March 2003: 4–6.

Kitchen, P.J. and Schultz, D.E. (2001), *Raising the Corporate Umbrella: Corporate Communications in the 21st Century*, Palgrave: London.

Kotler, P. (1980), *Marketing Management*, 2nd edn, Prentice Hall: Upper Saddle River, NJ.

Kotler, P. (1986), 'Megamarketing', *Harvard Business Review*, March–April, 117–124.

Kotler, P. (2000), *Marketing Management* (millennium edn), Prentice-Hall Inc.: Upper Saddle River, NJ.

L'Etang, J. (2002), 'Public relations education in Britain: a review at the outset of the millennium and thoughts for a different research agenda', *Journal of Communication Management*, 7, 1: 43–53.

McArthur, D.N. and Griffin, T. (1997), 'A marketing management view of integrated marketing communications', *Journal of Advertising Research*, 37, 5: 19–26.

Newsom, D. and Carrell, R. (1986), 'Megamarketing (response)', *Harvard Business Review*, September–October: 170.

Pearson, C.M. and Clair, J.A. (1998), 'Reframing Crisis Management', *Academy of Management Review*, 23, 1: 59–76.

Perrault, W.D. and McCarthy, E.J. (1999), *Basic Marketing: a Global Managerial Approach*, McGraw Hill: Boston, MA.

Pickton, D.A. and Broderick, A. (2001), *Integrated Marketing Communication*, Pearson Education: Harlow.

Schultz, D.E. and Gronstedt, A. (1997), 'Making marcom an investment', *Marketing Management*, 6, 3, Fall: 40–49.

Schultz, D.E. and Kitchen, P.J. (1997), 'Integrated marketing communications in US advertising agencies: an exploratory study', *Journal of Advertising Research*, 37, 5: 7–18.

183

Shimp, T.A. (2003), *Advertising, Promotion, and Supplemental Aspects of Integrated Marketing Communications*, 6th edn, South-western/Thompson Learning: Mason, OH.

Therapeutic Goods Administration (TGA) (2003), Website listing all media releases and official product withdrawal notices, http://www.tga.gov.au. Accessed 1 September 2003.

7 Sponsorship

Brassington, F. and Pettitt, S. (2003), *Principles of Marketing*, Financial Times Management: London.

BSR (2003), www.bsr.org (accessed 23 August 2003).

Clow, K.E. and Baack, D. (2002), *Integrated Advertising, Promotion and Marketing Communications*, Prentice Hall/Pearson Education: Upper Saddle River, NJ.

Cornwell, T.B. and Maignan, I. (1998), 'An international review of sponsorship research', *Journal of Advertising*, 27, 1: 1–21.

De Morgen, 16 November 2000.

De Pelsmacker, P., Driessen, L., and Rayp, G. (2003), *Are Fair Trade Labels Good Business? Ethics and Coffee Buying Behaviour*, Ghent University Working Paper.

De Pelsmacker, P., Geuens, M., and Van den Bergh, J. (2004), *Marketing Communications. A European Perspective*, Financial Times/Prentice Hall: Harlow.

Duncan, T. (2002), *IMC Using Advertising and Promotion to Build Brands*, McGraw Hill/Irwin: Boston, MA.

Duncan, T. and Moriarty, S. (1997), *Driving Brand Value*, McGraw-Hill: New York.

Easton, S. and Mackie, P. (1998), 'When football came home: a case history of the sponsorship activity at Euro '96', *International Journal of Advertising*, 17, 1: 99–114.

Fill, C. (2002), *Marketing Communications. Contexts, Strategies and Applications*, Financial Times/Prentice Hall: Harlow.

Floor, J.M. and van Raaij, W.F. (2002), *Marketing-communicatiestrategie* (marketing communication strategy), Wolters-Noordhoff: Groningen.

Hoek, J., Gendall, P., Jeffcoat, M., and Orsman, D. (1997), 'Sponsorship and advertising: a comparison of their effects', *Journal of Marketing Communications*, 3: 21–32.

Johnstone, E. and Dodd, C. (2000), 'Placements as mediators of brand salience within a UK cinema audience', *Journal of Marketing Communications*, 6, 3: 141–158.

Lagae, W. (2003), *Marketingcommunicatie in de Sport* (marketing communications in sports), Pearson Education: Benelux.

Meenaghan, T. (1991), 'The role of sponsorship in the marketing communication mix', *International Journal of Advertising*, 10, 1: 35–48.

Meenaghan, T. (1996), 'Ambush marketing – a threat to corporate sponsorship', *Sloan Management Review*, 38, 1: 103–113.

Meenaghan, T. (1998), 'Current developments and future directions in sponsorship', *International Journal of Advertising*, 17, 1: 3–28.

Pickton, D. and Broderick, A. (2001), *Integrated Marketing Communications*, Financial Times/Prentice Hall: Harlow.

Shimp, T.A. (2000), *Advertising, Promotion, and Supplemental Aspects of Integrated Marketing Communications*, The Dryden Press: Fort Worth, TX.

8 e-communications

ACP (Association of Coupon Professionals) (2001), *A Guide to Internet Couponing*, www.couponpros.org.

Bhat, S., Bevans, M. and Segupta, S. (2002), 'Measuring users' web activity to evaluate and enhance advertising effectiveness', *Journal of Advertising*, 31, 3: 97–106.

Brassington, F. and Pettitt, S. (2003), *Principles of Marketing*, Financial Times Management: London.

Briggs, R. (2001), 'Measuring success: an advertising effectiveness series from the IAB', *IAB Europe*, 1, 3: 1–5.

Chaffey, D., Mayer, R., Johnston, R., and Ellis-Chadwick, F. (2003), *Internet Marketing. Strategy, Implementation and Practice*, Financial Times/Prentice Hall: Harlow, Essex.

Clow, K.E. and Baack, D. (2002), *Integrated Advertising, Promotion and Marketing Communications*, Prentice Hall/Pearson Education: Upper Saddle River, NJ.

De Pelsmacker, P., Geuens, M., and Van den Bergh, J. (2004), *Marketing Communications. A European Perspective*, Financial Times/Prentice Hall: Harlow.

Dwek (2002), 'E-mail in the UK overtakes snail', *Marketing Week*, 21 March: 44.

Elkin, T. (2003), 'Size matters, so does price', *Advertising Age*, January: 13.

Enpocket Insight (2003), *The Response Performance of SMS Marketing*, www.enpocket.com.

Euromonitor (2002), *European Marketing Data and Statistics 2002*, Euromonitor: Brussels.

Gaudin, S. (2002), *The Site of No Return*, www.cyberatlas.internet.com.

Huberland, X. (2003), *Developing New Services Based on Mobile Business: SMS/MMS Case: From 'Person to Person' to 'Mobile Business'*, Proceedings of the Mobile Marketing Congress: The Added Value: Brussels.

Keeler (1995), *Cybermarketing*, Amacon: New York.

Sen, S. (1998), 'The identification and satisfaction of consumer analysis-driven information needs of marketers on the WWW', *European Journal of Marketing*, 32, 7/8: 688–702.

Smith, P. and Chaffey, D. (2001), *e-Marketing Excellence: at the Heart of e-Business*, Butterworth-Heinemann: Oxford.

Smith, P. and Taylor, J. (2002), *Marketing Communications: an Integrated Approach*, Kogan Page: London.

Sotd (2003), *SnapNames State of The Domain Q1 Research*, www.sotd.info/sotd/memeberes.aspx (accessed 25 June 2003).

Tapp, A. (2002), 'Proactive or reactive marketing? The influence of the Internet on direct marketing, part 3', *Journal of Database Marketing*, 9, 3: 238–247.

Waring, T. and Martinez, A. (2002), 'Ethical customer relationships: a comparative analysis of US and French organizations using permission-based e-mail marketing', *Journal of Database Marketing*, 10, 1: 53–69.

Weima, K.W. (2002), *Webvertising. Tools voor een effectieve campagne* (Webvertising. Tools for an effective campaign), Kluwer: Alphen aan de Rijn.

9 Relationship marketing

Berry, L.L. and Parasuraman, A. (1991), *Marketing Services: Competing Through Quality*, The Free Press: New York.

Brassington, F. and Pettitt, S. (2003), *Principles of Marketing*, Financial Times Management: London.

Clow, K.E. and Baack, D. (2002), *Integrated Advertising, Promotion and Marketing Communications*, Prentice Hall/Pearson Education: Upper Saddle River, NJ.

Curry, J., Wurtz, W., Thys, G., and Zylstra, L. (1998), *Customer Marketing – How to Improve the Profitability of Your Customer Base*, MSP Associates: Amsterdam.

185

De Pelsmacker, P. and Van Kenhove, P. (2002), *Marktonderzoek. Methoden en toepassingen (Marketing research. Methods and applications)*, Garant: Antwerpen/Apeldoorn.

De Pelsmacker, P., Geuens, M., and Van den Bergh, J. (2004), *Marketing Communications. A European Perspective*, Financial Times/Prentice Hall: Harlow.

Duncan, T. (2002), *IMC Using Advertising and Promotion to Build Brands*, McGraw Hill/Irwin: Boston, MA.

Fill, C. (2002), *Marketing Communications. Contexts, Strategies and Applications*, Financial Times/Prentice Hall: Harlow.

Godin, S. (1999), 'Permission marketing: the way to make advertising work again', *Direct Marketing*, 62, 1: 41–43.

Gummesson, E. (2000), *Total Relationship Marketing. Rethinking Marketing Management: From 4Ps to 30Rs*, Butterworth Heinemann: Oxford.

Hartley, B. and Starkey, M.W. (1996), *Management of Sales and Customer Relations*, Thomson International Press: London.

Jenkinson, A. (1995), *Valuing Your Customers: From Quality Information to Quality Relationships through Database Marketing*, McGraw-Hill: London.

Jobber, D. and Fahy, J. (2003), *Foundations of Marketing*, McGraw-Hill: Berkshire.

Kotler, P. (2003), *Marketing Management*, Prentice Hall: Upper Saddle River, NJ.

O'Connor, J. and Galvin, E. (1997), *Marketing and Information Technology*, Pitman: London.

Pickton, D. and Broderick, A. (2001), *Integrated Marketing Communications*, Financial Times/Prentice Hall: Harlow.

Rapp, S. and Collins, T. (1990), *The New Direct Marketing. How to Implement a Profit-Driven Database Marketing Strategy*, David Shepard Associates: Homewood, IL.

Reichheld, F.F. (1996), *The Loyalty Effect. The Hidden Force Behind Growths, Profits and Lasting Value*, Harvard Business School Press: Boston, MA.

10 Summary and conclusion

Alderson, W. (1964), in Cox, R., Alderson, W., and Shapiro, S. (eds) *Theories in Marketing*, Richard D. Irwin, Homewood, IL, p. 101.

Carter, M. (2003), 'Audi UK' in *Creativity Works*, D&AD: London.

Kitchen, P.J. (ed.) (2004), *Marketing Mind Prints*, Palgrave: Basingstoke. In press.

Kitchen, P.J. and Li, T. (2004), 'Perceptions of integrated marketing communications: a Chinese ad and PR agency perspective', *International Journal of Advertising*, forthcoming.

Kitchen, P.J. and Schultz, D.E. (2003), 'Integrated corporate and marketing communication', *Advances in Competitiveness Research* (USA) 11, 1: 66–86.

Kitchen, P.J., Brignell, J., Li, T., and Spickett-Jones, J.G. (2004), 'The emergence of IMC: a literature review and critical commentary', *Journal of Advertising Research*, forthcoming.

Woolf, V. (1984), 'Modern fiction', in McNellie, A. (ed.) *The Common Reader*, first series, Harcourt Brace Jovanovich/First Harvest: London.

Index

Note: *t* or *fig* following a page reference indicates material in tables or figures

187